Also by Gale Sayers

I AM THIRD *(with Al Silverman)*   1970

FOOTBALL.

Bob Griese

A N D

Gale Sayers

To my wife, Judi, and my mother. For their patience.
BOB GRIESE

To all youngsters, playing everywhere.
GALE SAYERS

Photographs by Henry Fichner

Foreword

To become a professional football player requires total dedication: It is such a long way from a boy's backyard to the Orange Bowl on a Sunday afternoon. Between the two places are a lot of stops—junior high school, high school, college. Along the way, as a boy becomes a man, he acquires the tools he needs to become a good football player.

Bob Griese, of course, has made all the stops and gone through the entire progression and is now at the top. Early he learned by trial and error. Later, he had proper coaching. But at every level, he must have approached his football lessons with thoroughness and dedication, the same way he approaches his work as a quarterback. From what I can see here, he approached this book with Gale Sayers in the same manner.

I'm not sure that any instruction book can make a football player out of a boy. It takes more than words and pictures to accomplish that job. But a youngster needs fundamentals to start him on the right foot. This is what this book by Bob Griese and Gale Sayers offers best of all—fundamentals.

From the first chapter, when Bob describes how to set up to receive a snap from center, to the last, where he discusses establishing command presence, he takes the young player step by step through a short course in how to prepare himself to play a demanding and exciting and thoroughly satisfying game.

I've said it many times, and I'll probably be saying it many more. Bob Griese is an excellent pro quarterback. Before he has finished his career, he may well be ranked among the greatest of all time. Already he has taken his team to the Super Bowl. To get there, he was toughened in the fire of that grueling play-off game with Kansas City on Christmas Day, the longest and the most exciting game I've ever seen.

Gale Sayers? What more can be said about him? Year after year, before he injured his knee, he was the most feared runner in the game. I have seen him do everything—return kicks for touch-downs, break away on long runs from scrimmage. He was the Chicago Bears' most explosive and most deadly weapon.

He is a fundamentally sound player. In many ways, although I do not know Gale nearly as well as I do Bob, they are similar. Both are quiet, preferring to lead by example. Both are totally committed to excellence.

I think you may find some of that philosophy here in this book.

DON SHULA
Coach of the Miami Dolphins

Contents

ix

Introduction

IT WAS JUST BEFORE the Super Bowl last
year, and Bob Griese was alone with a friend in his
room on the eighth floor of the Fontainebleau Hotel
in New Orleans. Bob had brought the Dolphins
through twenty-two games to this climactic con-
frontation with Dallas, some of them almost un-
believable—the heart-stopping 27–24 win over
Kansas City in the play-offs in a game that went
nearly six quarters, the longest in football history,
the regular-season, come-from-behind 24–21 win
over Pittsburgh, when Bob had come out of a sick
bed to earn and win National Football League
Player of the Week honors.

He was twenty-six years old, and the best quarterback in professional football. Already for the

1971 season he had been named the American Football Conference Player of the Year and, naturally, the best quarterback in the conference. And after the Super Bowl he would be going to the Pro Bowl in Los Angeles as the starting quarterback for the AFC.

He was rooming alone before the Super Bowl, just as he does on most road trips, and for practical reasons. While the other players watch television or rap with each other, Griese watches the opponent's game films, playing them over and over, forward and backward, looking for some flaw he can exploit during the game. In his Fontainebleu room, the only piece of nonhotel furniture was the sand-colored movie projector next to his bed.

Outside, eight stories below his private balcony, was the hotel pool, occupied by two live dolphins imported from Mississippi, perhaps to make the Miami Dolphins feel at home.

Bob stepped to the window and idly watched the dolphins at play in the pool. The biggest game of his life was barely seventy-two hours away, but he didn't want to talk about it. He preferred instead to talk about his childhood, about teaching himself to play football because there had been no coaches for his age group at home in Evansville, Indiana.

"Our grade school didn't have football," he said. "Only basketball and baseball. We had real good basketball coaching in the winter, and in the summer there was Little League baseball, so we got coaching there. But no football. Even the parents didn't help us much. Maybe they didn't know that much about the game.

"We learned on our own, kids my age—nine, ten, eleven, twelve years old. We never had a regular field to play on. We would play in somebody's yard, or down at the lawn in front of the city library. It was always a sandlot situation.

"So as far as learning how to pitch or how to shoot a basketball, we were in good hands. But learning how to carry a football or run with it or tackle somebody, we had to pick up on our own.

"I remember playing in the side yard of our house, which was very close to the house next door. The side yard between the two homes was no more than thirty yards long and perhaps ten yards wide, and more often than not this was the football field we played on. It wasn't easy to get around anybody and run for a score because the field was too narrow. So the games were made up of throwing. Almost every play was a pass, which forced me to perfect my passing. Besides, runs were dangerous. Both houses were made of brick, and the bricks on the house next door were very rough and coarse. If you got too close to the house with the coarse brick, you could scrape your face badly. Too close to my house and you might take a fall on a concrete sidewalk that ran the length of the field.

"I know there were no books in the library or at school to help me learn football. Nothing instructional for a boy my age, nothing by anybody who really knew what he was talking about, and especially nothing with illustrations. I wish there had been. It might have saved me a lot of trial and error. At the time we didn't know how to throw a football. We just took the thing and slung it sidearm. The ball always was too big for us to handle. Now I know a youngster can't pick up the biggest ball around and expect to throw it properly. You progress as you grow. I should have started off with a smaller football, something my hand would fit."

Bob was the youngest in the neighborhood. His brother was two years older, but even so Bob joined the older crowd for sports. At the time it was tough on him, since he was smaller and at a disadvantage. But the experience and the training of playing with older kids accelerated his development.

"I think this is the reason I learned so quickly.

Primarily I learned by watching older fellows and picking up how they did it. A lot of my learning was by sight, no matter whether it was right or wrong. All I knew was if the guy went down it was a good tackle, and if the pass went for a touchdown it was a good pass. There was no way of knowing if the technique was correct. Learning to catch was just pitch and catch. We didn't know about looking the ball into our hands or working on any of the standard receiver drills they have now.

"Being the smallest, I took more punishment than anyone else. This was only natural, since physically I couldn't compete with kids two years older than I was. I started wondering if football was always going to be this rough, I mean too rough for me. But later, when I began playing with kids my own age, the lessons I learned from older kids put me a step ahead—a little better runner, a little better passer, a little better blocker."

Now, of course, Bob has children of his own— two boys, the eldest not yet in first grade. In his spare time he plays ball with them. Pitch and catch mostly, or a scaled-down scrimmage of two against Dad. Most children, unfortunately, don't have football's best quarterback to play with them. So they'll have to learn the way Bob did, but with

5

the advantage of having Bob tell them how with text and pictures. It's sort of like having the best of Griese at your fingertips.

In 1971 Bob had a splendid season. He completed 145 of 263 passes for 2,089 yards and 19 touchdowns. He was intercepted only 9 times. And those figures do not include his play-off accomplishments—a touchdown pass each against Kansas City and Baltimore. After only five years as a professional, his Dolphin records show 760 completions, 77 touchdown passes and 10,281 yards gained passing. Three of those years were before Don Shula became head coach, and before the Dolphins were even remotely a championship contender.

He came to the Dolphins from Purdue in 1967 as Miami's number-one draft choice. At Purdue he was an all-American quarterback, and took the Boilermakers to the Rose Bowl championship in 1967 with a 14–13 victory over Southern California. As a college sophomore in 1965 he engineered a Purdue upset over Notre Dame, 25–21, completing a remarkable 19 of 21 passes. "It was the greatest exhibition of passing I have ever seen by any quarterback," said Ara Parseghian, the Notre Dame coach.

He was second to Steve Spurrier in the Heisman

Trophy voting as College football's Player of the Year in 1966. Even so, the Dolphins planned to draft Griese ahead of Spurrier, although Spurrier attended the University of Florida and was a strong local favorite. "I knew who I wanted from the first," said Joe Thomas, the Dolphins' player personnel director at the time. "I was going down the line with Griese. I'm only glad San Francisco took Spurrier before it came our turn to choose. I'd hate to have had to explain to the hometown people why I passed up the Heisman Trophy winner for the best quarterback in football."

Don Shula, the Dolphin coach, considers Griese unequaled among the pros. "He has everything you could ask of a quarterback," Shula said. "Intelligence, a good arm, durability." Totally confident in Griese ability, Shula lets Bob call all the plays during a game. "I trust him completely," Shula says. "His judgment is beyond question. And as he matures, he can only get better and better."

And already he is the acknowledged best in the league—the AFC Player of the Year in 1971.

Look at Gale Sayers' records and you understand why he is considered perhaps the greatest natural runner in the history of the National Football League. And that includes guys like Jim Brown and Leroy Kelly, too. In just under five complete seasons, he holds nine NFL and sixteen Chicago Bear team records. Five times, from 1965 through 1969, he was a unanimous all-League running back. He has been named Most Valuable Player in the Pro Bowl three times, and he has rushed for more than a hundred yards a game twenty times.

All this, even though he has had to miss more than two seasons because of injury. With five games remaining in the 1968 season, Kermit Alexander of the San Francisco 49ers made a clean tackle on Gale in Chicago. Gale went down, and couldn't get back up. His right knee was damaged, and he underwent surgery the next day. But he came back the next year to win the George Halas Trophy as the NFL's Most Courageous Player, gaining more than 1,000 yards and making all-League again, which had become almost standard with Gale Sayers since he came to the Bears in 1965 as a shy rookie from the University of Kansas.

In 1970, however, Gale missed nearly the entire season, this time to undergo surgery on his left knee. And then, last year, after fighting his way through the Bears' training camp and most of the regular season, Sayers was forced to miss still another regular season for more surgery. Now, finally, the doctors believe he can be the old Gale Sayers again, the man who looks as if he moves on ball bearings, so smoothly does he run.

Gale Sayers, as most of us know by now, is more than simply a superb football player. His unique humanness surfaced sharply in the spring of 1970 at a dinner in New York, after which he was to be given the Most Courageous award. Brian Piccolo, his friend and roommate on the Bears since 1967, was dying of cancer in a New York hospital. Gale had given blood and friendship and support, but was powerless in the face of the cancer.

He had wanted Brian to go to the award banquet with him, but that wasn't possible. So Gale accepted the award, and immediately announced he was passing it on to Brian.

"You flatter me by giving me this award," he said, "but I tell you here and now that I accept it for Brian Piccolo. Brian Piccolo is the man of courage who should accept the George S. Halas award. It is mine tonight, it is Brian's tomorrow. . . . I love Brian Piccolo and I'd like all of you to love him, too. Tonight, when you hit your knees, please ask God to love him. . . ."

Three weeks later, Brian Piccolo died.

Gale grew up in middle America—Kansas and

Nebraska. He lived as a child in Wichita and, later, in Speed, Kansas. His companions were always his brother and a few close friends. They taught themselves to play football. There was no Little League for them, no organized programs. From Speed the family moved to Omaha, Nebraska, and that's where Gale Sayers began to make a name for himself.

His grade school athletic program was as good as a high school program in many cities. He ran track. He played basketball and baseball. He played football, but, oddly, in light of what he was to become in the pros, he played middle linebacker. By the time he completed high school in Omaha, he had seventeen college scholarship offers. He selected Kansas, and as a sophomore he was an all-American, in spite of Kansas's ordinary record. By the time he completed his senior year every pro team was seriously interested in making Gale Sayers the first draft choice.

This was a time when the American Football League was at war with the NFL. Kansas City of the AFL drafted Sayers. In the NFL, the choice was between San Francisco, Chicago, and New York. The 49ers took Ken Willard. The Giants took Tucker Frederickson. And the lucky Bears got Gale Sayers, at six feet and 200 pounds the most explosive runner the league has ever known.

In five years he scored 56 touchdowns, 22 of them as a rookie in 1965. He gained more than 1,000 yards in 1966 and did it again in 1969, coming off the knee surgery. The National Football League records he holds are: most touchdowns in one season (22 in 1965); most touchdowns as a rookie (22 in 1965); most touchdowns in one game (6 against San Francisco in 1965); most touchdowns on kickoff returns, career (6); most points rookie season (132 in 1965); total offense in one season (2,440 yards in 1966); total offense average one game (19.6 against San Francisco in 1965); kickoff return average (30.56).

That game in San Francisco was mind-boggling. Gale gained 336 yards rushing, catching passes, and returning kicks. His six touchdowns included runs of 80, 21, 7, 50 and 1 yard, and an 85-yard punt return in the fourth quarter. George Halas, the coach, said it was the greatest performance he had ever seen on a football field.

Since then Gale has proved over and over that he is one of the great running backs of all time. Only twenty-nine, and moving into his eighth year as a Bear, there is no reason to suspect he will not lead Chicago to the heights again. Every year he has played he has been an all-League selection;

11

and his string of five straight was broken only by the injuries of 1970 and 1971.

Gale Sayers and Bob Griese. The two best at their positions. In the following chapters they have boiled their game down to the essentials. Offensive football begins with the fundamentals. . . .

Stance and Posture of the Quarterback under Center

BOB GRIESE

WHEN I BREAK the offensive huddle and come to the line at the start of a play, the first defensive person I'm conscious of is always the other team's middle linebacker. Why? Well, one reason is because he usually has his eyes glued on me, looking for some clue, some small hint I might accidentally give that would tip the play.

Sometimes I lock eyes for a moment with Mike Curtis of the Baltimore Colts or Dick Butkus of the Chicago Bears or Dan Connors of the Oakland Raiders. I can almost feel them trying to read me. Pass or run? Will he sprint out or drop back? Is the play going to the left or the right? Will he call on Jim Kiick or Larry Csonka? Is Mercury Morris in there as a decoy, or will he get the ball?

My first job at the line of scrimmage is to give those linebackers nothing. Getting free information from me should be just as tough as breaking into the secret vault in the Central Intelligence Agency.

This is just one reason why the stance and posture of the quarterback under center in a T formation are so important. There are plenty of others. You have to be relaxed. You have to keep yourself tall so you can see what the cornerbacks and the safeties are doing. You have to be aware of the position of your feet so you don't get tangled up and fall on your face getting out of there to start a play.

First of all, don't tip the defense to run or pass plays. Your feet give you away more than anything else. Position your two feet a shoulder-width apart in an even stance. Don't put one foot behind the other if you plan to drop back for a pass. It won't help you get out from under center any faster, and it will be a sure sign to some alert defender that you're planning to throw.

When your feet are positioned, flex your legs slightly at the knees. Stiff legs are for flamingos, and when you have stiff legs you move about as

This is the correct stance from the side and front for a quarterback taking the ball from center. The quarterback is in a minimum crouch to ensure a quick getaway after the snap.

well as one. No football player should have his knees locked at any time, and that goes double for the quarterback. He has to be able to move out fast.

Place your hands under the center's rump, right hand on top if you are a right-handed passer, left hand on top if you throw left-handed. Spread the fingers of your upper hand, and keep the fingers relaxed.

The heel of the upper hand goes against the heel of the lower hand, forming a sort of "V" to receive the ball. Both hands should be relaxed. Relaxed hands accept the ball easily, almost like having the ball slide into a glove. Stiff hands yield sprained fingers and fumbles.

Keep your back straight and your head up. You want to be in position to see everything from your widest wide receiver to the deepest safety. You've seen pictures, or perhaps high school games, in which the quarterback was scrunched way down under the center. Forget those guys. By the time they unwind themselves they could be wearing a 200-pound linebacker around their necks.

Be relaxed up there. Turn your head from side to side, and keep your eyes looking from one side to the other. Don't fix your gaze on where you plan to throw—that's a sure tip-off—but keep your eyes

Waiting for the snap from center, the quarterback's hands and fingers are relaxed and spread with the heels of the palms touching.

roving. You know what you're going to do. The defense doesn't. Make them sweat it out.

In a passing situation, the quarterback should be concerned with getting away from center as fast as possible. This is one of the points I always look for when I'm watching a quarterback in action. How fast does he get out of there? How much time does it take him to set up to pass? The more time it takes to get back and get ready, the less time is left to find the target and throw.

If the play is going to be a run, the quarterback should consider himself simply an agent whose job it is to deliver the ball to the running back with the least amount of effort on the part of the back. After all, he's the man who is going to do the work. After you give him the ball, your job is finished. And you should get the ball to him as deeply as possible in the offensive backfield so he can concentrate on his blocking and on a hole opening for him.

If you, the quarterback, are sloppy in your work, if you don't get back to the point of hand-off rapidly enough or you make a poor hand-off, then, just maybe, the running back will be distracted enough to miss his cut or miss using a good block. The running back didn't kill the play. You did.

The only way to insure that your are prepared to do your job properly at quarterback is to assume the proper stance and posture at the outset. Don't get tangled up under center. Remember:

1. Position your feet a shoulder width apart and even; flex your knees.

2. Position your hands, heel touching heel, beneath the center in a relaxed fashion; relax your fingers.

3. Keep your eyes and head moving. Don't tip the play.

4. At the snap of the ball, move out fast.

The Grip

BOB GRIESE

IN MANY WAYS, throwing a football is a lot like writing with a pen or playing the saxophone or even tying a bow in your shoelace. In all of these exercises you use your fingers, not the palm of your hand. If you can imagine the difficulty of playing a tune successfully with the palms of your hands, then you've got a general idea of how tough it is to throw a pass with the football resting on your palm.

There are plenty of reasons for forgetting your palms. Can you impart spin with them? No. Can you throw a spiral without spin? No. And if you can't throw a reasonably good spiral, you're in trouble as a passer. The spiraling action produces two things—accuracy and distance. You put one of those wounded ducks into the air, wobbling and flapping, and some fast cornerback is going to pick it off for an interception. I know. It's happened to me.

There are exceptions—everything has at least one exception—to this "rule of the fingers." When the ball is wet, and only when it is wet, should you consider resting it on the palm of your hand to throw. The reason is simple enough. If you hold a wet ball in your fingers, it can easily slip out, squirt out. But how many times do you play on a wet field? Maybe one or two games a year. So don't worry about palming a pass now. Learn to pass with your fingers.

The problem many learning passers encounter is starting with a football too big to handle. If your hand isn't fully developed yet, don't practice with an official National Football League ball. It's too big. Find a football your size, one you can handle easily, one you can throw with your fingers. Master the art on this ball, and you'll be ready when the time comes to move up to the standard size.

Don't worry about your hand being large or small at this stage, The size of your hand is relative. It's the position of your hand on the football that counts. Passers with smaller hands hold the ball nearer its end, and vice versa. I have a small hand—at least I consider it small—and it doesn't seem to have hampered my career yet.

The fingers of your hand should be spread an inch to an inch and a half apart, and over the end of the football on the laces. The thumb should be opposite them, on the other side of the ball. Hold the ball with your fingers, as I've said, and not the palm of your hand. You should be able to hold it in an overhand passing position and see daylight between the palm of your hand and the ball. If you can't see daylight, you're palming it.

Your little finger and ring finger should be placed on the laces. You never want all your fingers off the laces because you cannot control the ball that way. Place your index finger near the point of the ball. This is important because the index finger is your control finger. The middle finger should rest comfortably about halfway between your index and ring fingers.

Okay, you're holding the ball with your fingertips. Now I don't mean to say you hold it so tightly that your fingers ache or the blood drains from the tips. It should be held firmly, but not so tightly that you feel uncomfortable. You should be able to hold the ball easily at your side, with your arm hanging loosely. You should have complete con-

The position of the fingers on the laces in my standard grip.

trol, but your arm or forearm should never feel sore from the tension of holding the ball.

There is no difference in your grip for different types of passes. You hold it the same way for short ones as you do for long ones. Inexperienced players often make the mistake of palming, or forcing, a long pass. This kind of habit can only lead to trouble later, so learn to hold the ball the right way from the start. You must build from a solid foundation.

I might say just a word here on getting the ball from center. Your center should know that when the quarterback takes the snap the laces should be somewhere on his right hand. He should not have to revolve the ball in his two hands, searching for the laces, while he's dropping back to pass.

Don't worry about jamming a finger or two while you're learning. I've had sprains more times than I care to remember. The only ones that really bother you are a sprained thumb or index finger because, as I said, these are your control fingers. Sprains to the other three can be overcome with adhesive tape and gritted teeth.

What about that exception? The one time you palm the ball? On a wet field, operating with a wet ball, I kind of palm it and "wing" it. You can't throw it with your fingertips from an overhand

Notice carefully how in these two pictures the palm of my hand does not touch the football. This grip guarantees full control with the fingers.

position because the ball will squirt out of your hand like a watermelon seed. So you come a little sidearm with the ball, about three-quarters to the side, and "wing" it.

All right. Let's go through the basic steps of the grip:

1. Hold the ball in your fingers—little and ring finger on the laces, index finger controlling at the point, middle finger midway, and thumb on the other side.

2. In passing position, you should be able to see daylight between the palm and the football.

3. Hold the ball firmly, but don't try to squeeze the air out of it.

Setting Up

BOB GRIESE

A QUARTERBACK can have the finest football mind in the world. He can be a superb play caller. He can be the slickest hand-off artist in the game. But if he can't pass, then forget it. No ability in a quarterback is as vital as his ability to pass.

Passing is a little more than standing up and ripping off a thirty yard spiral. If you don't "set up" properly, you'll never have time to launch your beautiful spiral. Setting up is one of the keys to becoming a successful passer.

How important is it? Let's see. When the Dolphins were driving for a berth in the 1970 NFL play-offs, we came to Atlanta for a crucial Monday night game with the Falcons, a team without much offense but possessing a fierce defense. The ground that night was soggy from an all-day rain, and I wasn't paying as much attention as I should have been to what I was doing.

I started to backpedal away from center, looking from right to left to find my receivers. I lost my footing, slipped, and fell flat on my back. The next thing I knew I had about half a ton of defensive linemen all over me.

I wasn't picking up my feet. I wasn't thinking. So what happened? I end up on my broad backside in a crucial game, on national television, with twenty million people watching. The down was wasted, our chance was gone, we had to punt—all because I hadn't set up properly.

Now, let's find out how to do it.

The first thing you must do when you take the ball from center to begin a running play is to bring it in close to your body. You wheel and deal from here. You don't swing around with the ball in an outstretched hand waiting for some pulling guard or faking fullback to knock it loose. You hold it in close, offer it for a fake, and then pull it back to your body. Or you give the ball to the back.

For a pass it's different. You take the ball from center and bring the ball to shoulder height, keeping both hands on the ball. Have it ready for release. You should have been adjusting your hand to the laces from the instant you take the ball from center, so that when you reach the passing area you're ready to throw. Don't wait until the last second to establish your grip.

You can drop back to pass two ways—direct backpedal or turn from the hips down and run sort of sideways, the way most quarterbacks do, crossing your legs over. The big thing to remember, no matter which method of dropping back you prefer, is to keep your eyes looking downfield. Never turn your head away from the developing action. A lot of times the defense will change at the snap of the ball: a receiver could fall, a defensive back could fall. You want to know this instantly.

It is most important to get back as quickly as you can. The faster you set up, the more time you have to throw. But keep your body under control.

When you have retreated the proper distance (this varies, and will be covered in later chapters) you plant your right foot. This isn't planting your foot to pass, this is the brake. You stop yourself cold. Then you take a step up with your right foot and one with your left and *then* throw.

Sometimes you see a quarterback pressed by the defense into throwing the instant he plants his back

I use two methods of setting up to pass. The first in this sequence is the cross-legged method, in which the body is turned to one side.

foot to stop his momentum. When this happens, you'll almost always see an underthrown pass.

When backpedaling, the easiest way to get the most speed backward is to hold the ball in your two hands in passing position and rock your arms in a back-and-forth motion. This helps you get better movement backward. You should not be leaning back from the waist up, which will increase your chances of stumbling. The best way is to keep your center of balance directly over the balls of your feet with your upper body leaning slightly forward.

The final and perhaps most important step in setting up is moving into the pocket, and I can't emphasize this enough.

Normally, defensive ends are told to charge from the outside, hemming in the quarterback. The offensive tackles blocking them should carry the ends to the outside, away from and behind the quarterback. So if you go deep and plant your right foot to brake, then take two steps forward, you are helping to form your own pocket by moving into the protected area at precisely the same time your blockers are moving defenders away from you.

No matter which method you chose, the direct

Here I drop straight back from center, always facing the defense.

backpedal or the sideways run, your goals are always the same:

1. Get the ball to shoulder height quickly, passing grip in place, ball held in both hands.

2. Maintain balance and control at all times, but move as quickly as possible.

3. Keep looking downfield. Be alert to the changing defenses and the developing pass pattern.

4. Plant your braking foot solidly.

5. Move up two steps into the pocket and hit your target.

Throwing

BOB GRIESE

THROWING. This is your number-one tool as a quarterback. Master the art and you're a winner. If you can't—well, maybe you're a better linebacker than you thought you were. There isn't a big secret to throwing passes—anybody can do it —the trick is doing it properly. And, as in anything else in life, you have to ground yourself in the fundamentals and then practice, practice, practice.

I can't emphasize practice enough. You can study passing all you want, but without the constant application of your lessons you'll never be able to do it well.

I remember when I was growing up in Evansville, Indiana. I don't know how many thousands of passes I threw before I even got to high school, but it must have been more than a hundred thousand. When I couldn't find someone to play catch with, I went out and worked on my own, throwing the ball and then retrieving it myself to throw again.

Remember the instruction on the grip, how you hold the ball in your fingers and not the palm of your hand? Here's why. When you throw a football, you release the ball in this sequence, all, of course, done so rapidly it's practically a single motion. First the ball leaves your little finger, then your ring finger, then your middle finger and thumb. The last finger to leave the football is your index finger—the control finger. The index finger guides the ball and imparts the spin.

Many times, however, when the flight of the ball is wobbly, the reason lies, not in your finger action, but in your wrist action. Your wrist often determines how well the ball travels, and perhaps your wrist was too loose or too stiff.

It's impossible to tell you exactly how stiff or loose to hold your wrist. Everybody is different, and this is where practice comes in. You must throw and throw and throw until you find what is right for you. Eventually it will come, if you grip the ball and release it correctly.

The position of the shoulders on release is important. They should be square to the target. As much as possible, you should be facing the receiver to whom you are throwing. It is naturally much easier to throw to the right if you're right-handed than to throw to the left. If you throw to the left, you must turn your whole body to get your shoulders square, since it is all but impossible to throw across your body.

Your feet should be positioned so that you step toward the target. You cannot turn your shoulders toward the target without adjusting your feet. If you are a right-hander throwing to your left, you must turn your shoulders and feet so your body faces in that direction. Do not step across or throw across your body.

Always throw the ball with an overhand release unless you are forced to do otherwise. An overhand release gets the ball up as high as possible, out of trouble and over the heads of defensive linemen. The only time I ever throw a pass sidearm is when I'm forced into it—a lineman is in my way, I'm about to be tackled, I'm desperate. The general rule in football is that sidearm passes are out.

The follow-through is very, very important. I can't emphasize this enough. You've seen a baseball pitcher on the mound follow through every time he throws. His arm goes all the way through and his leg comes right behind, so he's in position to field a batted ball. A quarterback must bring his leg through the same way. If you don't, you'll be throwing with your arm alone, and before long it will be sore.

Following through is important to the action of a spiral. The downward snap of your arm and the complete follow-through imparts spin to the football just as you would spin a globe or a free-turning bicycle wheel. The complete follow-through keeps your fingers in contact with the football until the last fraction of a second, insuring the spin needed to throw spirals.

I want briefly to mention throwing into the wind, which is a bugaboo for many young quarterbacks. A stiff wind in your face is nothing to fear if you know what to do about it.

In throwing into the wind it's important to have good form on release, producing your wind beater, a good spiral. Don't try to throw harder. Keep the same motion, use follow-through. Give the ball good momentum, but *don't* jerk your motion. Try-

From setup to follow-through, I keep my eye on target and hold the ball high.

The follow-through is complete, which is necessary to impart velocity and spin.

ing to throw the ball a mile against the wind is going to produce nothing but wobbly passes and lost
velocity. Be smooth and achieve a spiral.

You want the nose of the football up when
throwing into the wind. If the nose is down, wind
resistance increases and cuts distance. A nose-up
pass seems to ride the wind. Again, this requires
steady practice.

So, remember:

1. The index finger (control finger) imparts
spin. It leaves the ball last.

2. Set your shoulders square to the target.

3. Throw with an overhand release.

4. Follow through on every pass.

5. Practice, practice, practice.

Throwing on the Run

BOB GRIESE

THROWING ON THE RUN is not nearly as difficult as people make it out to be. Done the right way, it's really very simple—and very effective, I might add. Why throw on the run? Well, it gives the defense one more thing to worry about, because when you move the defense moves. It offers a different and often more favorable blocking angle for offensive linemen. And if you're a little on the short side, it gets you out and away from those giant defensive linemen.

There are so many times when I've used the running pass effectively, in all kinds of weather, that it's difficult to recall a single big play. I do know

One of the most effective plays is the running pass. This sequence shows how important it is to loop back from the line of scrimmage and run toward the target, shoulders square, before releasing the ball.

that it is invaluable when I'm faced with a particularly hard inside rush.

Just as in the straight drop-back method of passing, your shoulders must be square to the target. Naturally, it is easier to keep square if you are a right-hander running to the right than a right-hander running left.

The first thing you want to do if you're sprinting out is to get depth. By that I mean you don't come right out from under center and head for the sidelines. This will take you away from the target when the time comes to throw. You want to get seven or eight yards deep right away, running in a sharp arc away from the line of scrimmage. When you have reached seven or eight yards deep, and you see what the defense end is doing, then start upfield, running toward your target. This way your shoulders are square.

You should be running toward the line of scrimmage, ball held high and ready to throw. When you roll to the left, the procedure is the same except that the arc away from and back to the line of scrimmage is a little sharper because your body turn, as a right-hander, must be more complete.

Now, when you're running toward the line of scrimmage and toward your receiver, or parallel to him, a question arises. Do you lead the receiver?

The answer is no. You only lead a receiver when you're dropping straight back and the target is moving. When you are both moving, you throw the ball *directly at* the target, leading him not in the slightest.

Because both you and the receiver are moving at very nearly the same speed, the ball you are carrying is moving just as fast as you are. When you release the ball, it will not only be going forward, but also sideways, at the same speed the receiver is moving. It's a simple law of physics that many young quarterbacks never seem to master.

I cannot emphasize this enough. On a running pass, when you and your receiver are moving parallel, *do not lead the target.* Throw directly at him. The same principle holds true if you are moving and the receiver is standing still. Throw directly at him. Only when you are stationary, and the receiver is moving, do you lead him with a pass.

When you are rolling out to begin your running pass, you should hold the ball, again as in the drop-back pass, as close as possible to the shoulder of your passing arm—and you should hold it in both hands. Don't wave it around like a flag, one moment down at your hip and the next moment over your head. That's for grandstanders, not to mention the fact that it increases the chance of

Although at first it is more awkward for a right-handed passer to throw on the run to his left, the principle is the same as going to the right. Notice how I have looped back and am running toward the target, shoulders squared, at the moment of release.

fumbling. The ball should at all times be gripped ready to throw.

As soon as you are ready to throw—receiver in sight, shoulders square, running toward the line of scrimmage—brake down slightly and bring your speed under control. This is another common mistake quarterbacks make. They do everything right, except they forget to brake down. Then they're confronted with throwing at full speed, a difficult task.

Slowing down just before throwing doesn't mean you take your time getting away from center, gaining your depth, and making your turn toward the line of scrimmage. The name of the play is "sprint out," so move quickly and under control. Don't glide away from center. Brake down just before throwing.

Mastering the running pass is important to any quarterback. Not only does it give you the key to making the sprint-out play, but it gives you a way of delivering the pass on a scramble, or busted pattern. Rarely do you have time to stop, set up, and throw with somebody like Dick Butkus bearing down.

Your approach to the running pass includes:

1. Getting depth leaving center.

2. Not throwing before starting upfield, shoulders square to the target.

3. Not leading a receiver if you are both running parallel. Throw *at* him.

4. Keeping the ball in both hands, at shoulder height.

5. Braking down before throwing.

Running:
Stance and Carry

GALE SAYERS

THERE IS SO MUCH MORE to running than just tucking the ball under one arm and taking off for the goal. If this were all there was to it, anybody with a fair amount of speed and a little courage could be a good running back. I don't want to fool you, though. Truly great running backs—guys like Jim Brown before he retired at Cleveland, and Leroy Kelly, who has gained more than 5,000 yards with the Browns—are born, not made. Some people have even said that it looks like I run on ball bearings. Well, I didn't teach myself to run that way. It's just the way I do it. It's natural.

Maybe everybody can't be great. But there is no reason why you can't be good, and you can be a good running back by working at it, by learning the fundamentals and mastering them. There is nothing difficult about learning what you must know to be a running back. The only thing this learning process requires is practice and application.

Even now, after being with the Chicago Bears since 1965, I'm still learning something new all the time. With me, the new things are mostly refinements of fundamentals, but they are still something I didn't have before.

Okay, first things first. If you're going to be a running back, you have to master a stance. A stance is simply a running back's ready position in the backfield while waiting for the ball to be snapped. There are two stances for backs, a semiupright stance and a three-point stance.

The semiupright stance is just what it sounds like. You have your two hands on your knees, looking straight ahead. Some professional teams use this stance, but not many. Its big advantage is that it allows the running back to better see what the defense is doing.

The most popular stance in all of football is the three-point stance, which is simply crouching with one hand on the ground in front of you to steady your body. The feet are usually spread about a foot and a half, with the right foot slightly

Here is the two-point stance, favored by some teams. Even here, in this more upright position, you can see that the weight is not on my hands and knees, which would give me a tendency to pitch forward.

Here is the classic three-point stance. I am well balanced. Notice how my weight does not rest on the left hand, but is, instead, on my feet.

behind the left. The right hand, in this case, would be the steadying hand.

Do not go down on your knuckles, but place only the fingertips of your right hand on the ground. That hand is not to bear your weight, it is simply to insure that you maintain balance, which is all important in the stance. As in the semiupright stance, keep your eyes straight ahead.

Why balance? Why keep your eyes to the front?

You must be balanced because the play could move in any of three directions—left, right, or straight ahead. If you're leaning forward on the knuckles of your right hand, how can you expect to move quickly to either side if the play demands it?

Always keep your eyes and your head facing front to prevent tipping the direction of the play. The defense stays up nights watching game films in an attempt to catch an offensive player looking at the place where he's going. This is all a defender needs to gain enough advantage to make sure you never find daylight. Never look at the quarterback. Never look right or left. Look straight ahead until the ball is snapped. After that, you're off to carry out your assignment.

Now that you're in your stance, how do you take the ball from the quarterback? Again, two ways—

ABOVE: *This is the folded-arms method of receiving a hand-off, preferred by most teams.* BELOW: *This is the scoop method of taking hand-offs. Few runners use it.*

the scoop method and the folded-arms method.

Few teams use the scoop method, but Leroy Kelly of Cleveland prefers it, so it can't be that bad. This method is simply holding both hands palm upward. The quarterback hands you the ball as if he were stacking a piece of firewood in your arms.

The most common method is the folded arms. The quarterback slides the ball into the running back's stomach, and the back then clamps down on the ball with his upper arm and hand and lower arm and hand. If you are taking the ball from the left, your left arm is across your chest, elbow high and out of the way, and your right arm is roughly at waist level. Reverse the position if you are taking the ball from the right side—that would be right hand across the chest, left hand across the waist. When the quarterback sticks the ball into your stomach, just fold your arms over it.

From that starting position, you can shift the ball either to your right arm or your left arm. When running to the right, tuck the ball under your right arm, keeping it as far away from a potential tackler as possible. When running to the left, keep the ball under your left arm. This accomplishes two things: it frees your inside arm to ward off tacklers, and it puts the ball as far out of danger as

Tuck the ball tightly under your arm, hand and fingers curled around the nose of the ball. This is the safest way to carry the ball on all runs.

possible. If you're running right and holding the ball under your left arm, you're giving that defensive man an open shot at causing a fumble.

Don't be a fumbler. It doesn't do any good to run eighty-five yards and then lose the ball on a fumble. Every aspect of carrying a football should center around the best way not to fumble.

Even in professional football, I still see runners carrying the ball under the wrong arm. And most of the time, these are the same guys who have chronic fumble troubles.

So, remember these basic things about lining up and carrying the ball:

1. In a three-point stance, keep your balance. Do not put weight on your steadying hand.

2. Keep your eyes and head to the front at all times.

3. Always maintain balance and be in control of your body.

4. Take the ball from the quarterback surely, either by scoop or folded-arms method.

5. Always carry the ball under the arm farthest away from the defensive alignment.

Running: Getting There

GALE SAYERS

NOW THEN. After you get the ball from the quarterback, what next? You run with it. But even though you're on your own in a sense, you're still following a loose plan. You're still exercising fundamentals. This isn't the hundred-yard dash. The object isn't to get where you're going in 9.5 seconds. The object is to get there, period.

There is a very loose term in football called "style." You've heard it, I'm sure. Gale Sayers has his running style. Larry Csonka has his. Norm Bulaich has another. My style is smooth and fluid. It doesn't look as if I'm working as hard as I really am. Csonka, now, is something else entirely. He powers his way to his destination. I mean, this man is a bull at his work. He'll run right over you. Bulaich combines a little of both—he's fluid, and he's powerful.

The point I want to make is that Larry Csonka could no more be Gale Sayers than Sayers could be Csonka. You cannot copy anybody's style exactly. It just doesn't work. It's far better to run the way that is most comfortable for you. This style is yours, and I guarantee that in the long run it will be the most effective for you.

It's like the baseball stance of a batter. Maybe Pete Rose can bat .350 from his stance, but it wouldn't necessarily work for Richie Allen. Allen has a stance of his own. So, remember. Run your own way. Be comfortable.

As a running back, the quarterback nine times out of ten is going to hand you the football. You take it either by the folded-arms or the scoop method. Your job is to reach the point of hand-off as rapidly as possible, but in getting there you must take short, choppy steps. I don't mean little bitty mincing steps, but I do mean don't try to make it to the quarterback in one long stride.

There is a solid reason for this. When you first get the ball, as I've said before, you want to be in control. The hole the blockers were supposed to make for you at the line of scrimmage might not be there. You must be prepared to slide either right or left, picking an opening for yourself. Vince Lombardi called this "running to daylight."

If you are going full steam straight ahead, taking long strides, it figures that you won't be able to change directions. But if you're taking shorter, choppy steps—still moving as fast as you can— you know you're in control of your body, and you can go in any direction you choose.

More times than I can remember with the Bears I've reached the line with the ball and found no hole where it was supposed to be. So I slid to the outside or the inside and broke the play for a long gain.

The ball carrier, when he breaks into the secondary, should be looking for two things: daylight and help in the form of a blocker. When you see a block thrown, change direction accordingly. If you see the defender being taken outside, then go inside. Sometimes you can even set up the defender for your blocker. Give a fake to put the defender in the blocker's path, and then take off in another direction.

Don't be one of those wise guys who always tries to outrun everybody, including his own blockers. The blockers are there to help you, and a good runner uses his blockers to the fullest.

Always be aware of your blockers. They don't

61

have to knock the other guy down to make a good block. All they have to do is be between you and him. It is up to the runner to use his blockers effectively. You watch Jim Kiick and Csonka with the Dolphins and you'll see what I mean. They constantly stay close in behind their blockers until the block is thrown. Then those guys take off. I do the same thing.

After you are past the line of scrimmage, you are into the secondary. Some men in pro football are known as good secondary runners. I'm one of them, and Leroy Kelly is another. Mercury Morris is another, and so is Mike Garrett. Being a secondary runner means that, when you get a little breathing space, you can take advantage of it.

Usually, when I feel myself breaking free of the ruck and the mire of the scrimmage pit, I try to cut for the outside because I know the fewest defenders will be that way. In the middle, defenders will be converging from all directions.

A good secondary runner must have one talent above all others. He must be able to accelerate. By this I mean he must be able to pick up speed rapidly once he clears the line. A lot of big backs simply can't do this—they're running at maximum speed from the beginning. I've always been fortunate in that I have speed in reserve. In the secondary, an extra fraction of a second may mean the difference between being tackled and breaking free for a touchdown.

In the secondary, think of acceleration and sideline. One more thing handy to have in the secondary is that "sixth sense." That's the feeling you have that something is going to happen. A good runner in the secondary—at least I'm this way—seems to have a feeling when he's going to be hit from a blind area. When I sense this, I clamp down on the football. I don't want to ruin a good run by fumbling.

Finally, you have heard of "second effort" in runners. This means one thing—determination. Second effort is just telling yourself that you won't be brought down by the first man who hits you, and then not being brought down.

All good runners—no exceptions—give second effort.

Keep these points in mind:

1. Keep your body under control with quick, choppy steps when approaching the line.

2. Slide left or right when the hole is plugged.

3. Always follow your blockers.

4. Accelerate in the secondary.

5. Run determined. Don't let one defender bring you down.

Blocking

GALE SAYERS

OKAY, SO NOW YOU THINK you know how to
run the ball. Good. That's the fun and glory part
of being a running back. The tough part is blocking. There comes a time when you're going to have
to do the dirty work to spring somebody else on a
long run. Learn to block and block well, and you
will understand what satisfaction an offensive lineman derives from football. It is the satisfaction of
knowing you have done your job and, in doing it,
contributed to the success of the play.

Seldom is a good block recognized. But once in
a long while a block—just one block—can make
somebody famous. It happened to Jerry Kramer, a
guard on one of Vince Lombardi's great Green

Bay Packer teams. Green Bay was playing Dallas for the National Football League championship. It was bitter cold in Green Bay, well below zero. With less than a minute to go, Bart Starr scored the winning touchdown on a one-yard quarterback sneak. Who threw the key block? Kramer, letting Starr slip past into the end zone. The picture of that block has probably been shown thousands of times.

Even in the days when the Bears' offense was built around the running of Gale Sayers, I still had to block when I wasn't carrying the ball. You play for George Halas, you have to block. I wasn't prepared for the blocking I had to do when I got to the Bears fresh out of the University of Kansas, but I had to learn fast.

I'm sure you've heard the saying that football is nothing more than blocking and tackling. This, basically, is true. If the defense tackles, then nobody scores touchdowns. If the offense blocks well, then there's no stopping it. Blocking is as vital to the offense as tackling is to the defense.

A back must block both in passing situations and on running plays. He has three types of blocks at his disposal: the head-up, standing block for pass protection; the drive block on running plays; and the cross-body block for running plays.

In pass blocking, the back must think of himself as a lineman. He's there to protect the quarterback. On that play, protection is his only job, and the success of the pass depends on the protection being sufficient.

As a blocker you must take the pass rusher head up, slightly crouched. The rushing lineman will usually be larger than you are, so you have to keep your feet, and keep fighting him. When he is close to you, make first contact with him. Don't wait for him to gather all his momentum and catch you flat-footed. He'll bowl you over. And keep your head up and your arms and hands to your chest. If you push the rusher with your hands, it's an illegal move and means a fifteen-yard penalty.

Don't flinch from the rusher, but meet him head up, arms in, and make solid contact. And, remember, always keep your feet. Don't go throwing yourself at the rusher's feet, hoping he'll trip over you. He won't unless he is hopelessly clumsy.

The drive block is used on running plays. It is the simplest of blocks because it is so natural. You run at the defender, head up, and simply drive your head into the man, forcing him down or out of the play. Ideally, you should hit your man from a crouched position.

66

The most common block for backs is the upright or head-up block. Here I take the ready position, crouched and balanced to fend off a pass rusher.

In the head-up and drive blocks, always keep your eyes open. If you close them, you can't adjust to any moves your man may make. Always keep your head up. This is important, and you must do it without exception. Putting your head down takes your eye off the man you want to block, and it leaves you open to injury.

The cross-body block is often used near the line of scrimmage. It is performed just as it sounds. You position your body across the path of the defender, driving into him. This block is often used as a screening block. You may end up on your hands and toes, crabbing, but you're still keeping your body between the ball carrier and the defender.

The two blocks you will use the most, however, are the head-up and the drive blocks. But no matter which block you use, the important thing is to do the job. When you don't have the ball, and your assignment is not carrying out a fake, look for somebody to knock down. No matter what you think, there will always be somebody who needs to be blocked.

Remember on blocking:

1. Always keep your head up.

2. Never leave your feet unless you're knocked off them.

3. Keep your arms in. Holding costs fifteen yards.

4. Keep your eyes open.

5. Make first contact with the defender.

Quick Passes

BOB GRIESE

THERE ARE SO MANY different types of passes that it is difficult to talk about each one separately. The techniques of throwing each pass, plus the situations in which they are effective, would fill a book by themselves. So I've divided passing into three basic throws: the quick pass, the medium pass, and the long pass. These three categories include the play-action passes, the sprint-outs, the flares, the screens, the bombs, the possession down throws. When you're thinking pass, you really have to think of the whole spectrum.

Let's start with the quick passes. I like to think of them as passes that keep the defense off balance. You can't live on a steady diet of quickies, but neither can you live on all long passes or all medium passes. Ideally, you want to be adept enough at all three. That way the defense can't cheat on a weak phase of your game.

The essence of the quick pass is the short dropback. You don't go nine yards deep, set up, and throw. Instead, you take three quick steps back from center and fire. Usually you are throwing over the middle to a tight end or wide receiver, who is maybe seven or eight yards deep and slanting across the field, or to one of your backs flaring out toward the sidelines.

Maybe the greatest quick-pass combination in the history of football was Johnny Unitas to Lenny Moore at Baltimore. Unitas, of course, is a master at getting rid of the ball, and Moore was exceptionally fast, and a very tough man to bring down after he got the ball. Unitas would take his three steps back, whip the ball to Moore slanting over the middle, then watch the secondary begin to sweat.

When I talk about quick passes, I mean just that —quick. The quarterback takes his three steps back and throws all within a second and a half of taking the snap from center.

For a quick pass, the offensive linemen use a different blocking technique from the one they use when the quarterback drops back nine yards. On the deep drop-back, the blockers will set up and fight the rusher to keep him away from the quarterback. On quick passes, however, the linemen set up for an instant, then chop the defender down, bringing him to the ground and out of the play completely. The lineman only needs to keep the defender down an instant—just long enough so the man can't get those big paws up to knock down your quick pass.

The Atlanta Falcons are a team against which we use a lot of quick passes. They have two big defensive ends in Claude Humphrey and John Zook, and both are tough. We know we're going to have a heck of a time keeping those guys out all night on medium and long passes, so we try to get rid of the ball as fast as we can against the Falcons.

These quick passes give the offensive linemen a chance to vary their blocking. They can do what we call "aggressive blocking"—firing out on the man and taking him down. It's a welcome break from having to step back and let the defender come crashing into you at full speed. Any time you can help your offensive lineman win his battle with the defensive linemen, you want to do it.

Quick passes are a great way to retain possession. Those second and 5 and third and 6 situations are ideal times to use them. Using them controls the game and controls the ball, and this is what you want to do. Nothing frustrates a defense more than to have the ball moved steadily on it— nothing big, but so steady defenders get the idea they can't stop you.

There are times, of course, when quick passes aren't such a good idea. When the defense plays bump-and-run is one time in particular. In bump-and-run the defender is playing very close to the receiver from the outset. Since he's right there, a quick pass isn't a great advantage. In fact, he might just intercept it a little quicker than he would a medium-range throw.

The defense is going to determine to a large extent your passing game. If you cannot get the time to throw long because of a hard rush, then you are going to have to rely on your quick passes, medium passes, and sprint-out passes. On the other hand, if you have a receiver like Paul Warfield or Bob Hayes or Lance Alworth, and you have time to throw long against a bump-and-run defense, then do it. A long bomb is called a bomb because of the great damage it does—not only the six points, but the demoralizing of the defense.

But when you're working with the quick-pass game, keep these tips in mind:

1. Take three fast steps on the drop-back.

2. Throw within a second and a half.

3. Send your receivers no farther than eight yards downfield.

4. Use the pass in ball-control situations.

Medium-Range Passes

BOB GRIESE

LET'S FACE IT. The pass that's going to make you or break you as a quarterback is the medium-range pass. Every quarterback can throw a short pass—it's almost like making a lay-up in basketball. Not everybody can throw long well, but you *can* get along without the deep threat if you are proficient in medium-range passing.

What is medium range? It varies from roughly twelve to twenty-five yards, although twenty-five is certainly on the deep side. These are the passes that win games for a quarterback, since you use them in crucial situations, like your third and 12 or third and 15. I like to go back over our charts after a game and see how many third and long yardage situations we converted into first downs. I know by now that if you can convert 80 percent of third and long plays into first downs, chances are you'll win.

I'm blessed with the best receiver in pro football —Paul Warfield. He can run any pattern and catch any pass, but I think he is at his peak on medium-range passes. Countless times I've gone to him on third and 12 or third and 15 and he has always managed to break free. He believes, you know, that if he can touch the football, he can catch it. He's right, too.

Perhaps you've seen the Dolphins play on television. If you have, then you know our style of offense is ball control, which means Jim Kiick and Larry Csonka doing a lot of running. But no matter how good they are, at times they're going to be stopped or we're going to have penalties or mistakes and we'll be faced with that third and 15 call. If we have a long drive, say eighty yards, you can almost count on two crucial long-yardage situations on third down. In 1971, when we reached the Super Bowl with a 12–3–1 record, we were highly successful on our medium passing game.

Certain types of medium-range passes go well against a zone defense, and other types are more successful against a bump-and-run coverage. Before you play a team you should find out all you can about what kind of pass defense it uses. In a zone defense the defenders have an area of responsibility—a portion of the field—they must cover. In bump-and-run the defender plays man-to-man with the receiver. If you know which you are going to face, you're that much better off. The Detroit Lions, for instance, mix it up. They play a zone on first and sometimes second down. On third down, they like to go to a man-to-man coverage, double-covering the best receiver. Of course, they have Lem Barney and Dick LeBeau at cornerback, and with two men this capable they can pick and choose defense.

In throwing the medium-range pass, drop back seven steps—which should be about seven yards—and do it quickly. Remember always, the faster you retreat to your passing position, the more time you have to throw. On passes of this distance, your receiver should be a fraction of a second from making his final break when you throw the ball. Ideally, the pass is on its way when the receiver turns to look for it. You've heard about timing between receivers and quarterbacks. Well, this is where you use it.

Be sure on your medium-range passes *not* to lob them or float them. A pass of this distance is in the air too long to float safely. Somebody might intercept. Put as much zip on the ball as you can, by which I don't mean to try to throw it through a brick wall, but to move it, clothesline it to your receiver. Be particularly careful of this on sideline or out patterns. When your receiver goes down and breaks for the sideline, the quarterback always, to some degree, will be throwing cross field. Don't hang the ball. If a cornerback intercepts, there's nothing between him and the goal except you, and you're out there for offense, not defense.

When you drop back your seven steps or seven yards, plant your foot, and step up into the pocket to throw, the timing should work out this way. The tight end should be twelve yards downfield and making his break as the primary receiver. Check him to see if he's open. Then read your flanker, who may be running a pattern fifteen to eighteen yards deep. He should be making his break right after the tight end. If both of these men are covered, your third and fourth receivers, perhaps a back coming out of the backfield, should be breaking open. Usually, though, you'll find that, if your first and second choices are covered, you're pretty well out of time to throw.

Remember, medium-range passes, used in situations calling for a gain of twelve to twenty-five yards, win football games week after week. This is how to throw them:

1. Drop back seven yards.

2. Deliver the football with authority.

3. Develop the timing between you and your receiver.

4. Know the defense, man-to-man or zone coverage.

Long Passes

BOB GRIESE

THE LONG PASS in football is more than simply an attempt at a quick six points, not that I'm not delighted to get all the quick touchdowns I can on long passes. The play is more than that. It is a complement to your vital short- and medium-range passing game. You *must* attempt a certain number of long passes during the course of a game, if only to keep the defense loose and worried. If, through studying charts of my previous games, an opposing set of cornerbacks discovered I never threw long, it wouldn't take them a minute to decide to play all our receivers tight, taking away our short and medium pass game.

So, whether you are a good long passer or not, you must throw them. Understanding this, the best approach is to learn to throw them properly.

First of all, you have to have the time to throw. Naturally, a long pass takes more time to develop than a short one. You must have confidence that your line can hold out the rush long enough for you to throw. Secondly, your receiver must have the speed to beat a defensive back. Thirdly, if the time is there, and the receiver is fast enough, the throw must be reasonably accurate.

A long pass doesn't have to be thrown with pin point accuracy. It must be "laid up" in a long, arcing-type pattern, and it has to be "laid out" so a receiver can run under it. Unlike the medium-range pass, which must be thrown on a line, long passes must be put up in the air. And, normally, if you are throwing to one of the wide receivers, the pass must be thrown to the outside.

What does this mean? Well, it's simple. If the receiver goes straight down the field, and the defender is covering him on the inside (the defender is farthest from the sideline), running with the receiver, the ball should be laid up high between the sideline and the line on which the receiver is running. Don't throw the ball "inside" the receiver. This will make him cross the path of the defender in an attempt to catch the ball. It makes a tough catch for your man, and an easier intercept try for the defender. So, when the ball is thrown, it should be given a lot of "air," or height, and it should be thrown to the outside.

Now, most important on long passes, the quarterback must "look off" the safety or the cornerback because these guys will play the quarterback's eyes. This means if you plan to throw to the receiver on the left sideline, don't look at him. Look the other way until the last possible instant. If you always look at your primary deep receiver, you'll have every defensive back on the field standing on his shoulders.

I remember once, four years ago, when we were playing the New York Jets in Shea Stadium. They had a cocky, veteran cornerback named Johnny Sample. He knew all the tricks. In watching films of him at work, I noticed he was keying on the quarterback's eyes and coming up with a lot of interceptions and crucial saves. He was reading the quarterback, looking directly at the quarterback and not the receiver.

As I said, I knew he was doing this. Right before the half we had the ball. Sample's main job was preventing the bomb and a quick score. He was covering Gene Milton, who was with us at the time. Milton was fast, a 9.3 man in the hundred-yard dash.

I got the snap and quickly set up for a deep pattern. I first glanced briefly at Sample, who was backpedaling with Milton and watching my eyes. Then I looked away from him to the opposite side. Sample was fooled. He relaxed, thinking I was going the other way, and let Milton sprint on beyond him. When I looked back toward Milton a second time, I could almost see Sample's eyes widen. He knew he had been had.

I just laid up the ball, and Milton, beating Sample by twenty yards, made an easy catch for the touchdown. I had set it all up by "looking off" Sample. You have to do the same over the middle on deep patterns. You must "look off" the safety, making him think you're passing in the opposite direction from your true intention.

You can't throw a long pass without making a deep set-up, and you must get back quickly because every split second counts here. Use your fastest drop-back, the one where you turn sideways and run back to the set-up point, which will be ten yards deep. Plant your right foot solidly, because you'll need all your power and leverage, then step up into the pocket to take advantage of the protective cup your offensive linemen and blocking backs

At the point of release for a long pass, the nose of the ball is aimed well up in the air.

At the point of release for a mediu range pass of twenty yards, the nose the ball is only slightly elevated.

At the point of release for a short p of ten or fifteen yards, the nose of ball is pointed directly at the target.

are forming for you. When you see your man, let it go.

Remember one last thing. On long passes, it's best to keep both of your running backs with you to block. If they become part of the pass pattern, you may be too short of blockers to buy the time you need to get off the bomb.

Review it this way:

1. You *must* throw long passes to keep the defense loose.

2. Lay the ball up high. Arch it.

3. Throw between the receiver and the sideline.

4. "Look off" the cornerback and safety.

5. Set up ten yards deep and step into the protective cup.

Pass Receiving

GALE SAYERS

THE FUNNY THING about catching passes is that it looks so much easier than it really is. You see a back swing out to the flat, look over his shoulder, gather in a pass from the quarterback, and run fifty yards for a touchdown. Then you think, "Hey, nothing to it." Well, you're wrong. There is something to it. If you don't believe it, just watch a pro football game any Sunday afternoon and count the number of dropped passes. You'll be surprised at how many you see.

I remember once breaking into the open against the Green Bay Packers in an important game a couple of years ago. There was nobody within five yards of me. Virgil Carter, I think, was quarterbacking the Bears at the time. I saw the ball coming down and I thought I had a sure touchdown.

I dropped it—right there in front of 50,000 people—and the walk back to the huddle was one of the longest of my life. I felt as if everybody was staring at me. And the worst part about the play was that the pass was perfect, right in my hands.

You know why I dropped it? I didn't keep my eye on the ball. I didn't, as we say in the pros, "look the ball into my hands."

Of all the things you want to remember about pass receiving, this is miles ahead of the rest. Always, always, always look the ball into your hands. Never take your eye off it, from the minute you first see it leave the quarterback's hand until you are holding it just as tightly and surely as if he had walked downfield and handed it to you.

When I was growing up and playing in high school, one of the drills we used was to paint the numbers one through five in a circle around the middle of the ball, then have the receiver who caught the pass immediately call out the number facing him on the ball. The purpose of the drill was to make us keep our eye on the ball. It worked, too.

I cannot put too much emphasis on this point. You will never be a receiver if you don't keep your eye on the ball, looking it into your hands.

You've seen how a lot of people who are ball shy try to catch footballs, the way they often flinch and close their eyes and reach out stiff-armed for it. Usually they don't catch it, and the reason is that they violate every rule of pass receiving at one time.

We already know that if they close their eyes they can't very well look the ball into their hands. The other two things they do wrong are to reach for it with their arms locked and with their hands rigid.

To be an effective pass receiver, you must have relaxed hands. If not, you are asking for the ball to bounce off your hands. If you have trouble relaxing, let your hands hang limply from the wrist and shake them vigorously. When the ball hits your hands, they should be as soft as fine glove leather.

Your arms must be relaxed, mainly because stiff arms are going to result in stiff hands. No way to avoid that.

All right. You have loose hands and relaxed arms. You can look the ball into your hands. What next?

88

Expect to be hit by a defender when you catch the ball. It won't always happen, but chances are you'll get hit a good deal of the time. If you expect it, your chances of fumbling or dropping the pass are that much less. The instant you have control of the ball, you should be determined that nobody and nothing will make you drop it.

After you catch it, then you're a running back again. Look for daylight. Head for it. Accelerate immediately to top speed. You will likely as not be surrounded by fast defensive backs—and, believe me, they'll be coming after you hard.

I try to make it a personal rule not to loop back toward the quarterback in an attempt to avoid tacklers. For one thing, I may be just putting myself closer to more defenders. For another, I'm moving away from the direction I want to go. And, for a third, I may just barely make the first down on the catch. By looping back to try to gain long yardage, I may be sacrificing the sure first down. After you catch the ball, head for the goal.

Finally, pass receiving is a specialty, like passing or punting or place kicking. Practice is everything. Practice, practice, practice. If you can't find somebody to play catch with you, then throw the ball up in the air and catch it yourself. If nothing else, you'll be getting the feel of the football. The

In this sequence, I have my hands relaxed and ready to bring in a pass, looking back over my shoulder for the ball. When the ball arrives, I look it right into my hands before starting to run.

more you handle it, the more familiar it will be to you.

You pass receivers should concentrate on these points:

1. Look the ball into your hands.
2. Relax your hands and arms.
3. Expect to be hit after catching the ball.
4. Move toward the goal after catching the ball.
5. Practice, practice, practice.

Pass Routes

GALE SAYERS

LET'S CLEAR UP a couple of minor mysteries about the terminology of the passing game. You always hear people talking about "pass patterns" and "pass routes." A lot of the people talking loudest don't know the difference between the two. If you expect to know what you're doing running out for a pass, then it's best that you know what you're talking about.

A pass pattern includes the pass routes of every receiver on a particular play. The pattern is something each receiver must follow to avoid running into one of his own teammates looking for the same pass.

A pass route is the path taken by an individual receiver. Often there are several pass routes within a single pass pattern. The tight end will run his route, the wide receivers will run theirs, and a back may run still another.

The important thing to remember as a pass receiver is to run your particular route exactly. This is important, because the quarterback is expecting you to be at a certain place when he's ready to throw. If you run the wrong route, chances are the quarterback won't have enough time to look all over the field for you. He may be buried under a ton of defensive linemen.

I'm sure you've seen this many times on television. The quarterback, with all the time in the world, throws a pass that misses his receiver by twenty yards, the ball bouncing harmlessly on the ground while the crowd boos what it thought was a poor throw.

Chances are the throw was perfect. What happens in most cases is that the receiver makes a mistake and runs the wrong route. The quarterback throws the ball where his receiver is supposed to be. If the receiver isn't there, well, naturally the ball is going to hit thin air.

When running a pass route, the main thing you must remember is to run the route exactly. If your

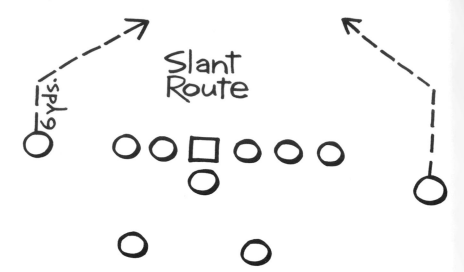

Slant Route: The receivers (dotted lines) go six yards before angling sharply toward the middle, where the ball will be delivered.

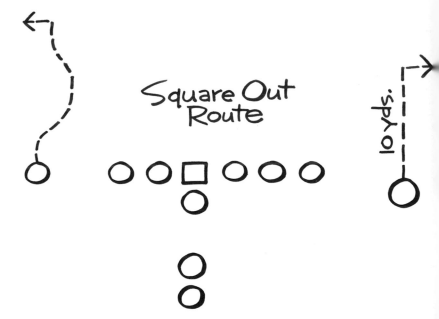

Square out Route: The receivers go ten yards downfield, at which point they cut squarely for the sideline. The ball is delivered at the cut.

route calls for you to go ten yards downfield and cut to the outside, then go exactly ten yards and cut. Not nine yards or eleven yards, but exactly ten.

Do not loaf on your pass route if you are not the primary receiver. All this does is tell the defensive back he doesn't have to worry about you any more. He can turn his attention to another receiver. Your job is to make the man covering you think that you are the primary receiver on every play.

When you run your route, run it briskly. Don't trot ten yards and then make a sprinting cut. The time you spend trotting must be subtracted from the time the quarterback has to throw the ball. Your job is to get to your assigned position—following your route to the letter—as quickly as you can. You want to be there when the ball is there.

What are the most common pass routes?

For a back, the most common routes are the flare or the swing. The back breaks toward the sideline, looping slightly so that his path describes a mild arc away from the quarterback. The quarterback tries to hit him with the pass as the back reaches the far end of the arc. As a general rule, the pass won't travel more than ten yards. The route is called flare or swing because the back is

95

"swinging" or "flaring" out of the backfield.

Another pass that backs must learn to handle is the screen pass. This pass is most often used when the quarterback is getting a hard rush. The offensive linemen usually only brush-block the defensive linemen, letting them through to pursue the retreating quarterback. As a running back you set yourself so it appears you are ready to block. Then, after a brief hesitation, you slip past the rushing defense and move to a prearranged spot on the field where the linemen—who, you remember, did not block the defense—are setting up a blocking "screen." The quarterback then delivers you the ball, a short pass, and you follow your blockers.

The difference between a screen and a flare is that the flare requires you to leave the backfield immediately. In a screen, you must hesitate.

Other routes are:

Post route—the receiver moves straight upfield ten or fifteen yards and then breaks on an angle for the goalpost.

Flag route—the receiver moves upfield ten or fifteen yards and then breaks for one of the flags in either corner of the end zone.

Circle route—the receiver comes out of the backfield and circles into the middle. A circle route

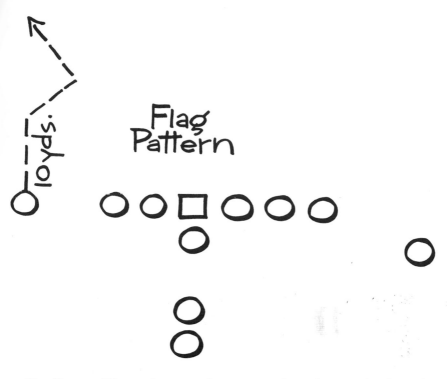

Flag Pattern

Flag Pattern: The receiver goes down ten yards, makes a cut inside, and then turns outside, angling for the flag that marks the corner of the end zone.

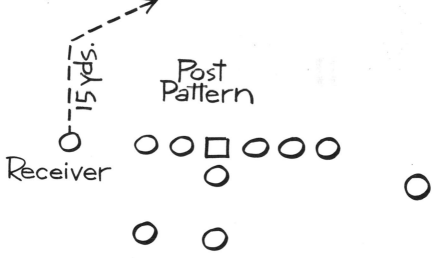

Post Pattern

Post Pattern: The receiver goes fifteen yards straight downfield and cuts on an angle for the goalpost, which is where the name post pattern originated.

could also have the back running up the middle and circling to the outside.

Square out—the receiver moves upfield a designated number of yards before planting his foot and cutting squarely for the sideline. This doesn't mean to round it off. The cut should be a 90-degree angle.

Remember these points on pass routes:

1. Always run the route exactly.

2. Always run as if you were the primary receiver.

3. Never break your route unless the quarterback is forced to scramble.

4. Move quickly to your assigned position.

The Halfback Pass

GALE SAYERS

I'm sure you've heard the term "triple-threat player." It means just what it says, although there aren't many players around today who can measure up to the designation. A triple-threat player is one who is effective running, passing, and kicking. Think hard for a minute, but I'll bet not one player will come to mind. Part of the reason is specialization. By the time a man reaches the pros, he's either a passer or a runner or a kicker. Sometimes two of the three skills are found in the same man, but it would be a miracle today to find all three.

The triple-threat designation sprang up in the years of single-wing football. The tailback handled the ball 80 percent of the time on a direct snap from center. He was, to be a good tailback, the team's best passer, runner, and kicker because it was up to him, in that offense, to do all three.

The best triple-threat man I can remember is a fellow named Dick Kazmaier, who played for Princeton in the early 1950s. He was an all-American, a fine runner, an adequate kicker, and, above all, the master of the running pass.

What a deadly weapon that running pass is! Sometimes it is called the halfback pass, but that is just to point out that the quarterback, in that particular instance, is not doing the throwing. Kazmaier became famous because he could throw the running pass better than anyone.

What is the running pass? Just what it says. You throw it on the run, not stopping to wind up and hunt for a receiver. If you're a running back who can throw the running pass, you will become such a threat you'll drive defenses nuts trying to think of ways to stop you.

In my years with the Chicago Bears I've thrown eighteen passes, which doesn't sound like many. But volume doesn't count here. Surprise does. I only wish I could throw it better than I do. The two best I ever saw in the pros were Frank Gifford, the TV announcer who used to play halfback for the New York Giants, and Paul Hornung, the former Golden Boy with the Green Bay Packers. Hornung was particularly effective, mostly because he was a quarterback at Notre Dame.

The halfback pass starts out looking exactly like a run, an end sweep. The key to its success is making it look like a run in order to draw up the defensive backs to make a tackle.

The quarterback generally will pitch you the ball as you flare for the sidelines. Tuck it under your arm, just as you would for a run, and keep it tucked there until the last possible moment. Don't run out waving the ball and telling the defense you're going to pass. Make the play look like a run and nothing more.

Your receiver—and usually it will be just one man—will first fake a block to confuse the defense even more. Then he'll slip out into the pattern. When you see him reaching his appointed spot, whip the ball into passing position and throw. Don't delay. Don't give the defense a chance to react.

Now, how to throw it. As a halfback you try to release the running pass the same way you would do if you were the quarterback. Square your shoulders to the target. How? Remember, you flared, or arc-ed, away from the line of scrimmage when the quarterback initially pitched the ball to you to start the play. If you kept on track in this mild arc, when the time comes to throw you should be running roughly at your target with your shoulders square at the man.

Most important. If the receiver is running a route parallel to your own, do *not* lead him as you would if you were standing still. With both of you running, throw the ball directly at the receiver. If you lead him, he'll never reach the ball. Remember. Throw the ball directly at him.

Of course, if the receiver is running downfield, then you must throw beyond him so he can run under the ball. Even then, throw the ball deep, but on the same line the receiver is following.

One of the beauties of the halfback pass is its effectiveness even if the play is fouled up. If your receiver is covered or falls down, the halfback pass simply turns into a regular, running sweep. If you see something going wrong with the pass play, fake the pass—put the ball up for the defense to see—and then tuck it back under your arm and take off.

The time to run the halfback pass must be chosen carefully. The defense must be "set up" for it. Usually the quarterback will have called several sweeps that look identical to the halfback pass.

When he thinks he has the defense properly lulled, he calls for the pass.

To be an effective executer of the halfback pass, remember:

1. Make it look like a run.

2. Flare away from the backfield in a slight arc.

3. Throw the pass on the run.

4. Keep your shoulders square to the target.

5. Throw directly at the receiver—do not lead him.

Scrambling

BOB GRIESE

"SCRAMBLING" MAY BE the most misunderstood term in professional football. Talk to five
different people and chances are you'll get five different definitions of the scramble, which basically
is simply what every quarterback does when he's
running for his life.

There are no planned "scrambles." There are
planned roll-outs, yes. A roll-out is a set play in
which the quarterback, rather than dropping back
to pass, rolls to one side of the field or the other.
More often than not he throws on the run. Scrambles are the original "save yourself, boys, the ship
is sinking" plays.

The scramble starts when pass protection breaks

down. It ends either when you're under 285 pounds of Bubba Smith or when you improvise well enough to make a successful play—run or pass— from a potential disaster.

People call Fran Tarkenton and myself scramblers when actually we're not. Both of us prefer the straight drop-back method of passing. I'd say 98 percent of Miami Dolphin pass plays are designed as straight drop-back, the other 2 percent being roll-outs. If I had my choice, I'd never scramble.

I recall that once, when we were playing the Baltimore Colts, protection for me broke down completely. I could feel Billy Ray Smith and Bubba and Ted Hendricks breathing their hot breaths right down the back of my neck. I ran at least four times from one side of the field to the other, using my blockers going each way and looking for a receiver. Finally, exhausted from the running and dodging, I just stepped out of bounds. I had used up so much energy escaping, I didn't have any left for throwing.

But that is a rare instance. The fact remains that, sooner or later in football, all of us quarterbacks are forced to scramble. Some do it better than others. Joe Namath, for instance, can't scramble at all. He has had so many knee operations he isn't mobile enough to run around back there. When his protection breaks down, or his receivers are covered, Joe throws the ball away. So does Roman Gabriel of the Rams.

As for me, I prefer to take the scramble and get what I can out of it, even if it's only saving my hide.

The key to a successful scramble is using your blockers. They are back there to help you, and it's up to you to use them to your advantage. If I'm forced to run to my right on a scramble, and I can't find my receiver, I loop back around to the left— looping rather deeply—so the friendly faces I left behind me can cut down on the defenders chasing me back across the field.

When you scramble you're on your own, in a sense, but you are always trying to find people to help you. Defensive backs, of course, hate to play against a quarterback capable of scrambling. While I'm running around looking for an open man, the defensive back is forced to cover a guy like Paul Warfield for eight or ten seconds. This is like asking him to grab a handful of quicksilver. Warfield has a way of slipping through your fingers.

At the outset of the scramble, your receivers will

do one of two things. They will break their normal pattern and run in the same direction you are running or, if tightly covered, they will break in the opposite direction, running away from you.

The second option presents difficulties. It forces you to stop, turn almost 180 degrees, square your shoulders, and throw—and do it fast. It is much easier to hit the receiver running in your direction, but this isn't always possible. Remember, if things were going according to your plan, you wouldn't be scrambling in the first place.

The roll-out is something else entirely. A team like Atlanta, one that rolls out often on a pass-run option, can cause headaches you wouldn't believe. I remember when we played Atlanta in 1970. Coach Don Shula worried all week about stopping Bob Berry and those darn roll-outs, so he drilled our defensive ends, Jim Riley and Bill Stanfill, steadily in rushing from the outside in order to force Berry to hold in the pocket.

A smart young quarterback should understand that a steady diet of scrambling is not going to produce a win. I think sometimes there is a strong temptation for young players to scramble just for the grandstand effect. They break out of a perfectly good pocket to take off on their own. About all this accomplishes is the busting of what might otherwise have been a successful play and the breaking down of your blockers' confidence.

Scrambling is a desperate maneuver. When you are forced into a scramble, try to remember:

1. Don't forget your blockers—they're still trying to help.

2. Loop back against the flow to set up blocks.

3. Move quickly, with the ball in throwing position.

4. Look for your receivers breaking with you or in the opposite direction.

Handing off
and Faking

BOB GRIESE

ON A RUNNING PLAY, the quarterback's only purpose is to get the ball successfully to the back who is going to carry it. Deliver the ball. Like the mailman, nothing must stay you from your appointed rounds. Why? You miss the hand-off and the back proceeds without the ball and you generally get mashed by a defensive lineman. Faking comes afterward, secondary to the 'true job of making sure of the hand-off.

As you learned earlier, the first thing you do as a quarterback when taking the ball from center is to pull it in close to your body. You don't want a pulling guard accidentally knocking the ball out of

ABOVE: *This is the folded-arms method of giving and receiving a hand-off. Most pro teams use it.* BELOW: *This is the scoop method of taking the ball on a hand-off. Here, the quarterback literally hands the ball to the runner.*

your hands when he bursts past you on his way to lead interference. Accidents have happened to the best of us. We forget to pull the ball in close, leave it hanging out from our bodies, unprotected— and, sure enough, the next thing we know it's gone.

Remember, bring the ball into your midsection and wheel and deal from there.

Now, at different times you fake with two hands and one hand. It is usually best with two hands, because this is the most natural way. You hand off with two hands, so it appears normal to the defense. If it is a fake, you hold the ball tightly in both hands, slip it into the stomach of the faking back, and pull it out. Do it quickly. Don't leave the ball in there to get knocked out of your hands.

On a one-handed fake, keep the ball cradled in your midsection with one hand, and offer the faking back a free hand. Do it quickly. Do it naturally. You're like a magician now. To the defense, particularly up front in the sudden confusion after the ball is snapped, the hand is much quicker than the eye.

Young quarterbacks should certainly begin by handing off and faking with two hands. It's safer. Youngsters often have small hands, which makes holding the ball in one hand tough.

When the play is developing, it is important for

the quarterback to stay out of the way. This is where timing comes in. When you arrive at the point of the hand-off, don't end up in the path of the running back. These guys can't change their route to suit you. Instead, you must regulate your speed to meet them at the convenient time. Arrive at the point of the hand-off as soon as you can, because if you're late the back must wait on you. He loses momentum, and often the hole that has opened briefly closes.

After the ball has been handed off, the fake becomes most important. You have heard of "play-action" passes. These are passes that come after a running play has been faked. Almost always, the quarterback calls the running play in advance of the pass, setting up the defense. When the actual running play is called, the quarterback should be sure to carry out the full fake, just as he would do if it were a play-action pass. The next time, if it is a fake run and a true pass, the defense will be momentarily confused by a good fake to the running back. This moment of confusion often is all the time it takes for a receiver to break free, and for the quarterback to hit him on a successful pass play. And it's all set up by a good fake at the start.

In bad weather, when the ball is wet and your hands are wet, the main thing to remember is to

stay under center a little longer. Be sure you have
the ball. When it's wet everything slows down—
the receivers, the line, the defense, the backs. You
have to adjust to this. Be sure you have the ball,
and be sure you deliver it where you are supposed
to deliver. A good habit is to fix your eyes on the
running back's midsection and keep them there until you see him take the ball from you. Deliver it
surely and firmly. Don't be a fancy Dan who slaps
it into the midsection as hard as he can. You're not
trying to knock the guy over. You just want to give
him the football.

Everybody doesn't take the ball the same way.
Some players want it stuck in solidly. Some players would rather have it handed to them.

I remember working in a Pro Bowl game with
Leroy Kelly of the Cleveland Browns. He didn't
want the ball in the conventional way. He didn't
lift his left arm high and keep his right arm low.
He kept both hands down around his belt buckle,
palms up. Instead of sticking the ball into a kind
of slot, as I do with Larry Csonka, I just handed it
to Kelly. It was like giving him a loaf of bread.

But these are things you learn as you go along
in football. Right now, it's enough to know how to
handle the basics properly. Don't forget your
basics:

1. Use two hands on the ball, faking and handing off.

2. On taking the snap from center, bring the ball quickly to your midsection.

3. Arrive on time at the exact point of hand-off, and plant the ball firmly.

4. Carry out all fakes. One play sets up another.

5. In wet weather, wait on the ball a split second longer.

Faking

GALE SAYERS

I THINK one of the most misunderstood parts of the game is the art of faking by a running back. In plenty of cases, the success of the entire play depends upon the success of the fake. In spite of this, too many halfbacks and fullbacks don't do their part when they don't have the football.

Every team runs some form of T formation now. They call them all kinds of Ts— wishbone T, veer T, split T, tight T, pro sets. But, basically, they all start the same way. The quarterback takes a snap from center and either hands off or throws to somebody.

That's the beauty of the formation and its variations. The play always starts the same way, a snap to the quarterback. He either gives the ball to the running back, or he fakes it and gives it to another running back on every running play.

It's easy when you're the back who gets the ball. You follow the basics of football, running as far as you can until somebody brings you down. But being the man making the fake is not so easy.

If you do your faking properly, you might get your teeth rattled by a jarring tackle. If you're concentrating on carrying out your fake, you never know what happened to the ball carrier because you're busy somewhere else trying to fool the defense.

In short, to my way of thinking, faking is one of the fundamentals of modern football. To do it and do it every play, you must be a team man. No matter what anybody tells you, football is still a team game—all eleven players involved, helping each other to help the team. If it weren't that way, why not play with ten? Because everybody is needed to do a job, and faking is a job.

Sometimes faking is only one part of a running back's job on a single play. I know, on the Chicago Bears, many times I'm what they call "the first back through the hole." The quarterback fakes to me and hands to the man coming through right after me—coming through the same hole. My job is first to carry out a good fake—to try to get myself tackled—and secondly to throw a block. Sometimes I have to block a linebacker by myself. Other times I help an offensive lineman with a defensive lineman.

But I do neither until I have first carried out my fake.

What does the fake do? Well, in the pros, where reactions and skills are the best in football, it serves to "freeze" a defense. This doesn't mean the defense stands stock still for a noticeable length of time. It means only that the linebacker or cornerback or defensive end is uncertain for a split second. He does not know where to go because he isn't quite sure where the play is going. Often this fraction-of-a-second freeze is all it takes to spring the ball carrier for a long gain.

The way you freeze a defender is to carry out a fake just as if you had the ball. The Kansas City Chiefs, I think, have more plays depending on fakes than any other team in football. Look at their success. They must be doing something right.

Where would a reverse go without a good fake? Nowhere. The key to making a reverse succeed is

One of the most often used fakes by a quarterback is the bootleg fake. Taking the ball from center, I run to my left, hiding the ball on my left hip until I'm ready to bring it to throwing position.

to convince the defense, even if only for a second, that the play is going in the opposite direction.

If you choose not to carry out your fake on a reverse, then you must think the defense is a bunch of rockheads.

It seems that every team has its prima donna, the star running back who doesn't want to block and doesn't want to fake. He isn't really a star, and he really doesn't understand football. If he did, he would know that he couldn't run five feet if his partner in the backfield didn't fake and block for him.

How long do you carry out a fake? You fake as long as you can. You fake until the play is over. How do you know when the play is a success if you're doing your job properly? You don't.

When the quarterback slips you a hand instead of the ball, go for that hand just as if it were the hand-off. When you're going out into the pass pattern, and you know you're not the receiver, make the secondary defender think you're the receiver. Keep him out of the play.

When faking, always try to:

1. Make the defense think you are the ball carrier.

2. Carry out the fake until the play is over.

3. Concentrate on this job just as hard as you would on carrying the ball.

4. Never expect the play to work without your fake.

5. Remember that all variations of the T formation require fakes.

Place Kicking

BOB GRIESE

PLACE KICKING is something not everyone can do. I guess it's sort of like being a high diver. Some guys work and work and work and still end up doing a belly flop. Same with kicking. But just maybe a lot of the kicking belly floppers started off on the wrong foot and never got straightened out.

But one thing is for sure. You don't have to be a monster to be a good kicker. Strength and size don't have nearly the bearing on successful kicking as does timing. Just look at men like Garo Yepremian, a successful kicker who is five feet eight and weighs 160 pounds with his kicking shoes on. Jan Stenerud of Kansas City is another one who isn't all that husky.

So this is one way for a little man to make it with

the big guys. All any coach wants to see is that ball go over the crossbar somewhere between the uprights. How big you are doesn't interest him in the least.

Don Shula, our coach with the Miami Dolphins, actually tells Garo Yepremian to stay out of the way after he kicks off. Garo's job out there is to kick the ball and avoid being hurt. We'll find somebody else to make the tackle.

I haven't kicked any with the Dolphins, but I could if I had to. For three varsity and one freshman year at Purdue I did all the place kicking and the punting, as well as the quarterbacking. And when I was a junior in high school I had already kicked a thirty-six-yard field goal in competition.

In college I kicked the winning field goal against Michigan—forty-eight yards—when less than five seconds remained on the clock. Even though I was six feet tall and weighed 180 pounds then, I was no giant. I did it with timing. And it wasn't just extra points and field goals, either.

I kicked off in every game as a sophomore, but our coach, Jack Mollenkopf, stopped me from doing that as a junior and senior. Some of the other teams started "headhunting" on me, trying to put me out of the game with a cheap shot. Anyway, I'm just trying to drive home the point that you don't have to be big to kick.

First of all, let's assume we're in a game situation. The ball should be held (remember, you can use some sort of tee at every level of football except professional) seven yards behind the line of scrimmage. This is far enough back to make a well-timed kick difficult for defensive linemen to block, and close enough to make the snap from center quick and sure.

I suggest that, when waiting for the snap from center, you fix your eye at the point where the holder will place the ball. There's no sense looking anywhere else. And, most important, when the ball is placed down, keep your eye on it.

Watch your toe hit the ball and, even after the hit, keep looking at the spot where the ball was. Don't look up to see if it goes through the goal posts. The noise of the crowd will tell you if it's good or bad.

Remember that in kicking this is the most important single thing. *Keep your eye on the ball.*

When you are lining up your kick, face the goalposts squarely so the path of the kick will take the ball dead center over the crossbar. You should be one and a half steps behind the spot where the ball will be placed. If you are right-footed, your right foot should be slightly ahead of your left.

From the rear, this shows the left foot at the moment the right makes contact on a place kick.

The toe of the kicking foot should hit this spot on the ball for a long kickoff. For an extra point, the kicker should aim slightly lower.

While kicking an extra point, keep your eye on the ball; never look up even after the kick is made.

When the ball is placed down, take a half step with your right foot, a long step with your left foot, and then swing through solidly with the kicking leg.

When waiting for the ball to be snapped, your body should be bent slightly forward, your arms hanging loose and relaxed at your sides. The ball is not snapped until you tell the holder, who is the man who gives the snap command, that you are ready. You control the play on this.

As I have said, keep your eye on the ball. I should go a little further and say keep your eye on the spot on the ball where you want your toe to make contact. For short kicks—extra points—you want to hit the ball low to gain height quickly. You don't need distance here. For longer kicks, raise your target area slightly more toward the middle of the ball. This will give you distance, but not as much height.

Now, after you have taken your short "jab" step with your right foot and your long "lead" step with your left, you should "lock" your right ankle as it swings through toward the football. By "locking" I mean make the ankle, foot, and lower leg one solid unit, which will give you power and assure a true kick, one that won't slither off to the left or right.

Even after you have kicked the ball, it is very,

Approaching the ball for a kick is important. Take your stance as in the first picture here, advance on a short step with your right foot, follow with a long step with your left foot, and then come in to kick with your right. Short step, long step, and kick.

very important to follow through, keeping your head down. So many kickers stop once their toe touches the ball, costing them accuracy and distance. After your kick is on its way, your right foot should end up on the ground in front of the tee, pointing toward the goal posts. In high school I always tried to pick up a blade of grass on the other side of the tee after the kick. This assured me of two things—keeping my head down and following through.

The big thing in place kicking, as it is in everything else, is practice, practice, practice. If you can't get a holder, then use a tee and kick by yourself. But keep kicking, kicking, kicking until it becomes second nature to do it right.

Remember these steps:

1. Line up one and a half steps behind the ball, right foot slightly in front of the left.

2. Take the first half step with your right foot, a long step with the left, and then swing the right foot through.

3. Lock your right ankle.

4. Keep your eye on the spot on the ball you want your toe to hit.

5. Follow through, head down, even after the ball is on its way.

6. Practice, practice, and more practice.

Kick Returns

GALE SAYERS

NOTHING TO MY WAY OF THINKING is as exciting as returning the kickoff for a touchdown. For sheer drama you can't beat it, and the psychological benefits are enormous. From a personal standpoint, it makes you feel like a superman. From a team standpoint, the lift of a quick touchdown is beyond measure. And the crowds— they love it. Besides, there isn't nearly the built-in risk you have on a punt return.

It you truly enjoy carrying the football, you'll love returning kickoffs. I've taken a lot of them back for the Bears, six for touchdowns. And it seems to me that the thrill is greater every time.

The kickoff return is simple. The defenders

usually aren't within thirty yards of you by the time you field the ball, so there's none of the pressure-building worry you feel on a punt when the defense has you almost surrounded. The kick itself is easy to catch, coming to you end over end without a great deal of height.

One thing is vitally important on kickoff returns. You must field the ball. Unlike a punt, the ball is not dead when a defender touches it. The ball is his. After a kick travels ten yards, the ball is called a "free ball," and any member of the kicking team can recover it. So remember—you *must* handle the football. You can down it in the end zone, but you cannot let it roll free.

I recall the classic incident of a man not fielding a kick. Warren McVea was the star runner for the University of Houston, which was playing the University of Miami in the Orange Bowl a few years ago.

After scoring a touchdown, Miami kicked off. McVea, in one of those inexplicable mental lapses, let the ball roll into the end zone. He retreated as he would from a punt, not wanting the ball to touch him.

The Miami kicking team thundered downfield and recovered the ball in the Houston end zone for a touchdown. Since the clock in college football does not begin to move until the receiving team touches the ball, Miami accomplished the rare feat of scoring twice with no time elapsed between touchdowns.

So, for goodness sakes, pick up the ball.

The elements of breaking a long kick return are simple enough. The deep-kick receivers stand, at least in the pros, on the goal line. In high school and junior high, they may be as shallow as the 20. Ten yards or so in front of them is what most teams call a "wedge." The wedge is made up of four players. Their job is to break open a vital crack somewhere in the coverage. When and if they do, you head for it.

To insure the wedge a chance to function, stay about five yards behind it until the members of the wedge have made their move. Do not run past the wedge until its members block somebody.

The kicking team usually comes down in what the defense calls "lanes." These lanes are nothing more than an imaginary path the defender follows downfield. Theoretically, if every defender stays in his lane and converges properly on the kick-return specialist, there can be no long return.

This is where the wedge comes in. It knocks somebody out of his lane, thus opening the way for you. Once you pop through that first wave of defenders, then turn on all the speed you have. Speed is everything on returning kicks. You never see a slow man back there, and the reason is obvious. You only get one, brief opportunity to take advantage of a key block. You have to be fast enough to go all the way once you get the chance.

There are three basic kick returns—the left side, the right side, and the middle. Most teams prefer to go straight up the middle. Since the defense is coming downfield more or less in a line stretching from sideline to sideline, the best way to get past them is straight ahead. Not only that, straight ahead is the shortest route to the goal. The time you spend running to the sideline not only gives defenders a chance to converge, it is time spent not moving downfield.

In any case, the direction of the return will be called in a huddle before the kick. Be sure you follow the plan. If the return calls for up the middle, and you decide to make it up the left sideline, your blockers will be of no help. So, don't try to be a hot dog. Stick with the plan. That's what it's for.

Finally, when you field the ball initially, don't dawdle getting to your wedge blockers. You want to be right there when a lane opens. If you're back on the goal and they throw a block at the 20, the

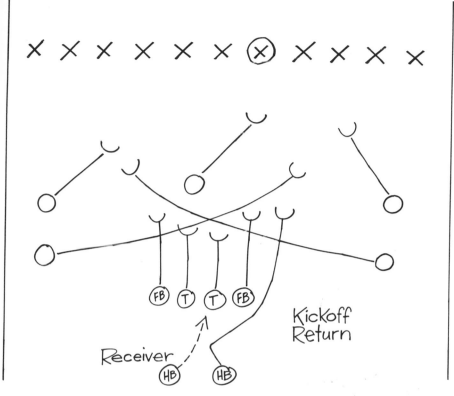

Kickoff Return: The wedge is clearly shown here, forming in front of the receiver. Also notice how wide men on the receiving team crisscross for better blocking angles.

defender will be back on his feet long before you can take advantage of the block.

The important points to remember in returning kicks are:

1. Always field the ball. It's in play.

2. Never overrun your blocking wedge before it has a chance to block.

3. Once through the line of defenders, accelerate.

4. Follow the planned route—middle, left, or right.

5. Move quickly after fielding the kick to be near your blockers.

Punting

BOB GRIESE

DON'T LET ANYBODY ever tell you punting isn't an offensive football weapon. It is, particularly in high school and college. Some of the most famous college coaches of all time—General Bob Neyland of Tennessee and Bobby Dodd of Georgia Tech—often punted on third down when they were deep in their own territory and far from the first down. The strategy is simple. If you have a tough defense, and your punter is measurably better than the other man's, then eventually through an exchange of punts you're going to improve your field position at his expense. This is why coaches like Dodd and Neyland always tried to have a punter who could drive the ball high and deep.

There's no big secret to punting. Anyone can do it if he's willing to devote time and practice to learning. As in passing, punting is mastered only by doing it over and over and over.

The basic necessity is a leg that is both strong and has good "snap" from the knee down. You don't have to be a big man. Look at Bobby Joe Green of the Bears. He can't weigh more than 170 pounds, but he's been one of the NFL's best punters for nearly fifteen years. Why? He has the snap, the strong leg, and the timing.

First of all, in a game situation, line up deep enough behind center. You might shave it slightly in a children's game, but in honest competition— high school on up—fourteen yards behind center helps insure that your kick won't be blocked. When the ball is snapped, make sure you catch it. Look it right into your hands.

Now then, you're back far enough and you know you must look the center snap into your hands. How do you punt?

Hold the ball lightly in two hands. This is no time to be a hot dog, so *use both hands*. When you make contact, your foot should be pointed almost like a ballet dancer's foot, and the ball should make contact slightly on the outside of your foot. This produces the spiraling action. To help achieve a spiral, I hold the ball slightly point down when I'm preparing to kick.

The drop of the ball is very important. You don't want to hold the ball high over your head and release it, because too many things can go wrong on a drop of this distance. Nor do you want to release about a foot off the ground. The ideal spot is just below waist high. The release should be careful so the ball falls just the way you want it to. When your foot swings through and makes contact, try to actually watch your foot hit the ball. This is the only way to be sure you're meeting the ball in the right place. You've heard men like Ted Williams in baseball talk about good hitters watching the bat meet the ball. Well, that's what good punters do—watch their foot hit the ball.

Take only the minimum number of steps to punt. Punters who take four or five steps before they kick are just asking to have the punt blocked. For one thing, it eats up precious time. For two things, you're walking forward, and that's where the defensive linemen are coming from.

At Purdue, when I was the team punter, I took the same number of steps to punt as I did to place-kick. I stood to receive the ball with my right foot (left foot if you're left-footed) slightly in front of my left. When I got the ball from center I took a short step with my right foot, a long step with my left, and then snapped my right foot into the punt.

Follow-through is very important. Follow-through gives you height, distance, and spiral. Don't just spank the ball with your foot and stop. The punt won't go anywhere. After your foot meets the ball, keep swinging through until your leg is at its fullest extension. If you watch professional punters, you'll see many of them actually leave their feet entirely at the very peak of their follow-through.

Height is more important than pure distance. Naturally, if a punter can kick high and far, he's that much more valuable. But a high thirty-five-yard kick with no return is much better than a line-drive fifty-yard kick that is returned thirty yards because the punt coverage didn't have time to get downfield.

When learning to punt, don't get fancy. The three steps you take should be taken straight ahead. I've seen people step sideways or walk in a curve or any number of things before they punt. Your three steps should be straight ahead.

So, when you practice, keep these steps in mind:

1. Hold the ball in both hands.

Starting the approach to punt, hold the ball at waist level. Drop the ball carefully from a point no higher than the waist in order to minimize the chances of a poor drop. After making contact follow through completely with your kicking foot. The follow-through supplies spiral and distance.

2. Arch your foot, pointing it like a ballet dancer.

3. Make a careful drop from slightly below waist high.

4. Meet the ball slightly on the side of your foot.

5. Take a short right-foot step, long left, and then snap into the punt.

6. Follow through completely.

Punt Returns

GALE SAYERS

THE PUNT RETURN is a double-barreled play in football. At least I like to think of returns that way. Pull the right trigger and you're a hero with a long return for a touchdown. Pull the wrong trigger and you're a bum with a lost fumble deep in your own territory. In either case, you are back there by yourself with every eye in the stands on you. So take the positive approach. Be a hero. Catch the ball. After that, start worrying about that long touchdown return.

In my years with the Chicago Bears, I haven't been the team's principal punt returner. But when I have had a chance, I've usually done pretty well.

I've averaged 14.48 yards per return, and two of my twenty-seven returns have gone for touchdowns, one an 85-yard run. The Bears prefer to have me returning kickoffs, but that's another chapter.

Obviously, the number-one objective in punt returns is to catch the ball. Most coaches have heart attacks waiting for their return specialist to make the catch. As I've said, a lost fumble on a punt usually means disaster.

As in anything, the way to learn to catch punts is practice, practice, practice. You can't expect to become an expert at it in one day after reading one chapter in a book. But there are fundamentals you can follow.

Always field the punt in front of you. Just like catching a fly ball, you want to avoid those dramatic over-the-shoulder catches if you can. You should try to catch the ball about at your midsection, making a kind of cradle with your arms and letting the ball drop into the cradle. Don't reach up to catch a punt with your two hands as you would catch a pass. It's too risky, so make the cradle. Take the punt and give slightly with it, sort of like rolling with the punch in boxing. Don't try to stand there like a brick wall. If you're that uptight, and that tense, you'll probably accomplish the same thing a wall would. The ball will bounce off you.

Always catch the ball with two hands. And I mean *always*. As in catching passes, keep your eye on the ball right into the cradle of your arms. Don't take it for granted that the ball will find its own way there. Look the ball into your arms.

After you catch the ball, the objective is to get to the outside and use the blocking of the protective "wall" your blockers should be setting up. Sometimes, in order to get behind the wall, you must loop back slightly, giving some ground. This, of course, is the ideal, but sometimes you won't have a chance to go anywhere except straight ahead. A lot of what you can do with a punt return depends on how good the defensive coverage is.

You should always fair-catch the ball if you know you're going to be hit immediately. This gives you a free shot at the catch, minimizing the chance of being jolted into a fumble. The fair-catch signal, you know by now, is one hand raised high over your head. When you signal for a fair catch, make it plain. It's up to you to tell the official and the defensive coverage what your intentions are.

Unless it is absolutely unavoidable, always catch the ball on the fly. If you don't, a good

I signal plainly for a fair catch before positioning my hands and body for a basket-style catch of a punt. See how I watch the ball all the way into my hands.

bounce for the punter could cost you fifteen or twenty additional yards. Even on short punts, run quickly to the ball and try to field it on the fly.

If the ball does hit the ground, stay away from it. All it has to do is nick you, and that's the same as a fumble. You'll be the only man on your team in the vicinity to recover a fumble, but plenty of guys from the other side will be there.

The first thing you look for after you field a punt is what your "short man," or the man who is your partner on the punt return team, will do. He must throw the first block for you. If the block enables you to head for the sidelines and the blocking wall, fine. If not, then you're on your own.

When starting out, one practice I would avoid in punt returns is fielding the ball with a running start. Nothing is more effective if it is done successfully, because you have a full head of steam when you catch the ball, but nothing is as risky. Your timing has to be perfect to pull off a stunt like this because you leave yourself no margin for error. I would field a punt on the run only if the Bears were desperately in need of a big return. Only then does the reward justify the risk.

When making a punt return you should:

1. Look the ball into your arms.
2. Always catch the ball in front of you.

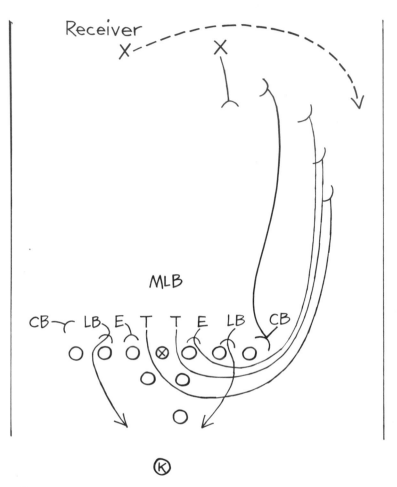

Punt Return: This is the classic "wall" punt return in which members of the receiving team peel back along the sidelines to set up a blocking wall for the receiver.

3. Catch the ball waist high, with your arms in a cradling position.

4. Always try to field the ball on the fly.

5. Signal for a fair catch in close quarters.

Strategy

BOB GRIESE

SOME SPORTS REPORTER long ago hung the title "field general" on a quarterback he fancied. Since then the term has been worked to death, but, no matter how old and hackneyed it is, it's accurate. On the field the quarterback is *the* man in charge. He devises the attack, he initiates it, and he controls it to the finish, just as a general would do in a military battle. Neither general nor quarterback can function without using strategy, which is nothing more than brainwork. The quarterback and the general who can think a little faster and and a little further ahead of the enemy are the ones who win.

The Dolphins were playing the Lions not long

ago on a hot August night in the Orange Bowl. We were trailing, 24–21, with eighty seconds left. The ball was near the left side of the field, making that side, as we say in football, the "short" side, since that sideline was closest to where the ball lay. I had noticed that Detroit double-covered the wide receiver on the "long" side of the field, figuring he was the more dangerous of the two wide receivers, since he had more room to maneuver. The short-side receiver got single coverage.

Naturally, I wanted to throw to Paul Warfield, our best, in this situation, so I purposely set him out on the short side, although I would not ordinarily do this. Howard Twilley was on the long side. Sure enough, Detroit double-covered Twilley, assigning only Dick LeBeau, an experienced veteran, to cover Warfield.

I don't think any man can single-cover Paul Warfield. LeBeau couldn't, and he's one of the best. Warfield broke to the outside, and I hit him in the end zone with a thirteen-yard touchdown pass. We won 28–24. A lot of the reason was because I could apply the right strategy at the right time.

I could give you a hundred more examples of strategy winning games, but I would rather tell you how to think strategy as a quarterback.

The basics should be obvious. Know your own

material. Who's your best receiver? Who's your best runner? Which offensive lineman is a weak pass blocker, and which one can blow a defender out of the way on a quick opener? You can't operate a car unless you know where the accelerator and steering wheel and the brake are. Neither can you run a team without understanding what makes it go, and what makes it stop.

Know your opponent as well as possible. Maybe you can match a strong blocker against a weak lineman. That's your advantage. Put your best receiver against their weakest cornerback. Look for injured or limping defenders. Look for players slow on their feet.

Strategy begins here. Know your material—and know the enemy's material.

If a play is working, keep using it. Don't stop something successful. Make them stop you. We have a man on the sidelines charting every play I run. When I come to the sidelines one of the first things I do is check with him to see what's working and how often. I want to know what plays are successful and keep running them. If one receiver is doing much better than another, you should keep using him until the defense is forced to change or to double-cover. Always know what you're doing and why you are doing it.

Mixing calls and changing cadence is another way to employ strategy to throw off the defense. Barking your signals in an uneven manner or bobbing your head erratically can draw the defense off balance. And remember—always vary the number on which you want the ball snapped. Never fall into the habit of starting a play on the same count every time. Pretty soon some smart defender will figure you out and come busting in.

It's most important to mix your calls. By that I mean don't always run on first down or pass on second down. Don't fall into the trap of letting the defense anticipate your moves. By the same token, don't waste your time trying to fool somebody in a situation where your chances are slim. For instance, on third and long yardage—fifteen or twenty yards—everybody knows you're going to pass. So get back and pass as efficiently as possible. Don't waste time on a play-action call, one that requires fakes to running backs. The defense knows you aren't going to run.

The opposite holds true on second and 2 or third and 2—short yardage situations. Use your play-action here. The defense is more than likely expecting a run, so it's set up to be foxed. With what we call "gimmick" plays—a reverse, the Statue of Liberty—the situation should call for a run. Don't try them on long yardage plays, because the defense is going to be laying back waiting for a pass and the reverse won't fool anybody. Call a reverse when you are faced with a hard rush. This way the runner leaves the defenders behind him.

The best approach, and this can't always be used, is to run when they expect you to pass and pass when they expect you to run. I know it isn't totally possible, but it's something to shoot for.

Know the tendencies of the other team—what it likes to do in certain situations. For instance, I know that Baltimore and Detroit like to blitz when they're behind or when the offense nears field-goal position. Since I'm aware of this, I like to call plays that are effective against a blitz—quick passes, for a starter. Once, against Baltimore, we crossed the 50 and moved to the Colts' 35. I knew a blitz had to be coming. They wanted us back out of field-goal range. So I called a play I knew was very good against a blitz and still sound if no blitz developed.

Sure enough, they blitzed. I hit Karl Noonan over the middle with a short pass, and he carried it all the way for a touchdown. The play broke Baltimore's back, and we went on to make the American Conference play-offs.

One more important thing on strategy, and this

comes under the heading of desperate strategy. When your pass protection has broken down, when do you throw the ball away and when do you eat it?

I throw it away only when I'm near enough to the end zone or sideline to be sure I can put it out of the reach of the defense. When I'm under heavy pressure at midfield—three or four linemen bearing down on me and no escape—rather than take a chance on putting the ball up for grabs on a throwaway, I prefer to eat it and take my punishment. Never throw the ball unless you are sure in your mind exactly where it's going.

When you are thinking field generalship:
1. Know your team.
2. Know the enemy personnel.
3. Don't call obvious plays.
4. If a play works, keep going to it.
5. Vary your cadence, mix your snap counts.

Diet and
General Health

BOB GRIESE

As a professional athlete, I use my body to make my living just as, say, lawyers and accountants use their minds or carpenters and electricians use their hands. It would be pretty silly for me to do anything that would reduce the efficiency of my body. I know it's a trite saying, but my body takes care of me as long as I take care of it.

In line with this thinking, I have three very hard and very fast rules:

1. I don't drink alcoholic beverages.
2. I don't smoke.
3. I would never think of taking any drug, either as a stimulant or a depressant.

Drugs, alcoholic beverages, and smoking, I think, will damage a body more surely than anything I can think of. Smoking and drinking cut down on your wind, your body control, your ability to function properly. In the case of drugs—of narcotics—who knows what it can do to affect your physical or mental ability? Contrary to information spread by people who really don't know, the professional athletes I know do not take narcotics and drug stimulants. Bennies or pep pills or whatever you call them do not help your performance. Anybody who smokes or drinks or takes a drug is just defeating his own purpose. An athlete wants to be *in* shape. Tobacco, alcohol, and drugs only ensure a body staying *out of* shape.

NOW FOR DIET. A healthful diet can vary greatly from person to person, but the basics are the same—plenty of meat and vegetables and salads and easy on sweets and desserts. Why? The meats and vegetables give you what you need to build your body and keep it functioning smoothly —like an automobile that receives proper care and uses the best fuel. Desserts might taste wonderful, but that's all they do except add soft fat where you don't need it.

When I was young I always had plenty to eat—

but I stuck with the meats and vegetables, and I steered away from the starches and desserts. Once I made up my mind to eat carefully, I never had a struggle resisting something I knew wasn't good for me.

Hand in hand with diet is physical activity. While I was careful to eat the proper foods, I was, and still am, very conscious of staying in good physical condition all year round. When the football season ends, I keep my body active. I stay involved in sports. My wife and I both play tennis often in the off season with Howard Twilley and his wife. Twilley is our split end opposite Paul Warfield. He isn't a big man as pro football players go, but he is always in absolutely perfect physical condition. He watches his diet as carefully as I watch mine.

Any good athlete should keep decent hours. He should get plenty of rest and sleep, since he should have a refreshed body, not a tired one. If you expect to perform on the football field, you have to get proper rest. It isn't fair to yourself to cheat your body. The only way to compete with the guy who wants your position is to keep yourself rested, refreshed, and well fueled with the proper foods. If you don't, then you don't want to be number one badly enough.

Treat your body as if it were the only one you've

got, because it is. This is the big thing. If you mess up your body or your mind, you can't get another one.

One of the truest sayings I know is that you never appreciate good health until you don't have it any longer. Set up training habits and running programs and exercise schedules. Adhere to them. You hear a lot about discipline these days. This is what discipline is—not somebody else making you do something, but you making yourself do it.

The five cardinal rules of keeping in shape are:

1. Don't drink alcoholic beverages.

2. Don't smoke.

3. Never take drugs.

4. Eat proper foods.

5. Get plenty of rest and exercise all year round.

Command
Presence

BOB GRIESE

COMMAND PRESENCE. Something hard to define because it may mean a little bit of everything to a lot of different people. To me, basically, it means holding control of a football team through leadership and respect. If you do not develop your own form of command presence, then somewhere along the line you're going to wash out as a quarterback. You must always remember that a quarterback not only runs the team in a physical sense, he also motivates it mentally.

In the huddle, the quarterback calling the plays must be the final and, for the most part, the only word. If he isn't, then the other players being told what to do aren't going to go to the line of scrimmage with the idea of getting the job done. The quarterback actually is an assistant coach on the field.

The quarterback should command attention immediately when he steps into the huddle, and if there is talking it should stop the instant he arrives. From the time we group for our huddle on the Dolphins, we have only thirty seconds to call a play and get the ball snapped, and in college the time limit is even less. So you can see the importance of controlling the other ten men waiting for your decision on what play to call.

When the quarterback calls a play, it should be in a tone of voice that says this play will be run, this play will work. He should never be indecisive or equivocal. He shouldn't use a tone of voice that indicates the play might not work or is just something that came off the top of his head.

Quarterbacks are all different types of people. Some are cocky and extroverted, others are quiet and introverted. But no matter what type they are, when they get into the huddle they all should be alike—demanding leaders, insisting on excellence and on getting the job done.

Off the field the introvert can go his way, the extrovert his way. Myself, I'm the type who is introverted and quiet. I enjoy my family and my family life. My idea of a big time is playing with my kids on an off day, or playing tennis with my wife. Others—Joe Namath, for instance—are more the extroverted type. They're flamboyant off the field. They attract attention to themselves as if they were magnets.

This is fine with me. I live my life, and they live theirs. The point I'm trying to make is that in the huddle we all must be the same if we expect to achieve results. Although I've never been in a New York Jets offensive huddle, I'd be very surprised if Namath's approach to establishing command presence and to calling plays differs greatly from my own.

As in any business, there is a right way to do things and a whole lot of wrong ways. I think any football man will agree that the way I suggest to operate in the huddle is the successful way. You don't think for a moment the Jets could move offensively if Namath cracked jokes between calling plays. By the same token, if I walked into the Dolphin huddle and called a play like some Caspar Milquetoast might, I could not expect positive results.

I can't help but think of Bobby Layne when I think of command presence. He played for the Detroit Lions in the 1950s, and was he tough! He was one of the last of the pros not to wear a face mask. He demanded respect more than any quarterback before or since, and under him the Lions won championships. He wasn't a picture-perfect passer, and he had a potbelly. And, like Namath, he enjoyed his good times off the field.

But his will to win was so great he convinced his teammates they could execute any play he called. He made things work because he made the Lions believe in themselves.

Bobby Layne had command presence. Joe Namath has it. John Brodie has it. Johnny Unitas has it. I know I have it. If you want to play quarterback, you develop it.

Remember:

1. Establish yourself as the man in charge of the team.

2. Be authoritative in the huddle.

3. Display confidence that every play will work.

BOB GRIESE

A 1967 graduate of Purdue University, Bob Griese has in five years become, in the eyes of many, the best quarterback in professional football. In 1971 he was named AFL Player of the Year. Don Shula, the Miami coach, considers Griese unequaled among the pros. "He has everything you could ask of a quarterback," says Shula.

GALE SAYERS

Look at Gale Sayers' records and you understand why he is perhaps the greatest runner in the history of the NFL. In just under five complete seasons, he holds nine NFL and sixteen Chicago Bear team records. Three times he has been named Most Valuable Player in the pro bowl. Gale Sayers' great humanity surfaced sharply in his first book, *I Am Third,* which told of his relationship with his friend and roommate, Brian Piccolo, who died of cancer.

BILL BONDURANT

Bill Bondurant, sports editor of the Fort Lauderdale *News,* has been writing about sports for eleven years. He is a graduate of the University of Florida.